Field Trials and Judging

Field Trials and Judging

by

Charles E. A. Alington
(1929)

with

Comments and Commentary

by

Susan Scales
(2000)

SWAN·HILL
PRESS

Original Text Copyright © 1929 Charles E. A. Alington

Commentary by Susan Scales © 2000

Field Trials and Judging was first published by *The Kennel Gazette* in 1929

First published in the UK
by Swan Hill Press, an imprint of Airlife Publishing Ltd

British Library Cataloguing-in-Publication Data
  A catalogue record for this book
  is available from the British Library

ISBN 1 84037 195 1

Typeset by Rowland Phototypesetting Limited,
Bury St Edmunds, Suffolk
Printed in England by St Edmundsbury Press Ltd,
Bury St Edmunds, Suffolk

Swan Hill Press
an imprint of Airlife Publishing Ltd
101 Longden Road, Shrewsbury, SY3 9EB, England
E-mail: airlife@airlifebooks.com
Website: www.airlifebooks.com

This book is dedicated to the memory of my
dear friend Alexander Peter Dick, a distinguished
physician, accomplished amateur,
and a true gentleman.

Acknowledgements

Grateful thanks to the following for their help in various ways:

John Buckland
John Darling
Keith Erlandson
Laney Knowles
Sonia Scales
Helena Shiffner
Wilson Stephens
Alice Taylor
Stanley Wood M.B.E.
Trevor Wood

Foreword

In up-dating Charles Alington's *Field Trials and Judging*, an acknowledged standard published in 1929, Susan Scales' objective has been to show how the principles and logic of that important between-the-wars book apply to the greatly changed context in which modern field sports now take place. She does this by quoting Alington's text and adding her own reflections.

The sound principles of field trialling and judging remain unaltered despite the passage of time, but it is important to retain a clear grasp of what these principles are, and why they were adopted.

A gundog Field Trial is not a race, but a canine competition decided by human verdict. There is no score sheet, and each dog competes individually on the particular ground allocated to it, assessing and dealing with it according to its eyes and nose. The judges reach a collective and united decision, and a Trial requires that competitors and judges must establish and demonstrate mastery of their respective skills and tasks. Today, an individual may possess both skills, since many judges are also handlers. Although Alington had been a competitor as well as a judge, he belonged more to the latter role. In his day, the judges and the judged formed two rather distinct communities – socially, financially and influentially. Today that distinction has disappeared, and a good deal can be said both for and against this development.

In recent times the extent of field trialling activity has greatly increased. The Kennel Club's records show that some 700 stakes are now run per season, compared with just 100 in the 1950s. This seven-fold increase indicates not only much wider participation, but reveals that the quantity of ground made available for Field Trials has increased in response to the growing demand. Whether the quality of much of this newly available ground is up to the standards of earlier times is another matter. The demand for trialling ground will continue for as long as gundog Field Trials are worth holding – and 'worth' is the definitive word. Alington's *Field Trials and Judging* was written to set out and uphold the important criteria of quality.

Although, in an ever more crowded and urbanised Britain, the increasingly popular sports of shooting and field trialling have outgrown the more 'natural' resources formerly available to them, the sports continue to rely upon purpose-bred and trained gundogs, albeit in somewhat changed roles. For example, modern game shooting is increasingly static and sedentary, with the walking of root and fodder crops by extended lines of Guns largely confined to East Anglia and parts of the North. The momentum of advancing lines, assisted by accurate marking and speedy picking-up, has given place to an emphasis on teams of Guns moving by vehicles from one drive to the next according to a carefully timed schedule. In its day, Alington's book greatly assisted the understanding and improvement of gundog work, and Susan Scales further promotes this in her recognition and explanation of the modern gundog's adaptation to contemporary shooting conditions and practices.

As shoots change, so also must the gundogs of the future. Already, Retrievers and their handlers fulfil the follow-up function of gathering shot game, while Spaniels' primary role is to find and flush game. As a test-bed for gundog work, Field Trials have helped not only to retain the sound principles as enunciated by Alington, but to assist and speed up the adjustments that have been necessary. Recognising that change has and will occur, Susan Scales has adjusted her masterly treatise to take account of the sporting realities which – for better or worse – form the backdrop against which it must be read.

WILSON STEPHENS

Contents

Introduction

The 'Alington Book' was first drawn to my attention by Wilson Stephens who told me that he always re-read it the night before he judged a Field Trial. It was subsequently lent to me by Peter Dick, who used to come and train his dogs with me, every week, out of the shooting season. After his death, his copy came into my possession and I feel strongly that it is worthy of a much wider audience.

It is undeniable that Field Trials have done a tremendous amount of good over the years towards the better training and handling of gundogs and the breeding of more easily trained animals. This process had already begun in Alington's time and he clearly recognised the fact. Judges in his day were honest and positive, even if sometimes mistaken in their actions.

However, more recently there has been a change in attitude to Trials, which is becoming more and more apparent. Competitors are keener on winning than ever before, at least partly because, even for amateurs, there is considerable money to be made out of stud fees and, to a lesser extent, puppy sales. This is especially true if the owner of the stud dog is prepared to accept any and every bitch without enquiring about hip and eye status, the reason for the owner wanting to breed a litter, whether there is someone at home all day to care for the puppies, and whether there are good homes waiting.

Nowadays even comparative newcomers are extremely keen to become judges. This is partly because they think that they will get better treatment from existing judges if they are going to have the chance to 'judge the judges' on some future occasion. They also feel that there is considerable kudos in becoming a Panel Field Trial Judge and cannot wait to begin climbing the ladder.

In an ideal world, judges would wish to judge for one reason and one alone, which is to put something back into the sport by helping to select the best dogs for future breeding. Unfortunately, however, most of them are only interested in reaching a result, not necessarily the right result. It is so much easier to put dogs out for minor mistakes than to keep them in and assess the whole of the work done during a Trial. We know that there are occasions when shortage of game creates problems, but not very often. Most Trials, if allowed, would almost judge themselves. The best judged Trials are likely to be those at which there are no gasps of amazement when the results are announced.

However, judges are human with all that that implies in the way of both imperfect integrity and genuine mistakes. It is hardly to be expected that the general standard of ability or honesty in the Field Trial world should be any higher than in the population at large. Backbiting, the favouring of friends and other less than ideal behaviour goes on in all human activities. There is no reason why Field Trials should be any different, but the consequences of bad or dishonest judging are more serious than a wrong decision at the village flower show.

This book is a plea for us to get back to positive, honest judging. I sincerely hope that it will not fall on deaf ears.

The text set in the serifed type and size as in this example is the original written by Charles Alington in 1929.

Susan Scales wrote the text in this style.

Chapter 1

How Field Trials are Conducted

Field Trials for Spaniels and Retrievers are organised and run by Societies, Clubs or Leagues formed for this purpose. As many owners of gundogs have never been present at a Field Trial, a short general description of a Retriever Trial may be of interest.

Spaniel Trials, which are conducted differently in some ways, will be dealt with later. As hardly any two Societies adopt exactly similar rules and regulations, the following account can only be taken as accurate in a general sense.

Nowadays societies are constrained by Kennel Club rules and regulations to follow more or less the same procedure, though there are minor individual variations.

All arrangements for a Field Trial are in the hands of the Committee, whose first business it is to obtain ground on which to hold it. When an owner of suitable ground, generous enough and keen enough on the improvement of our gundogs to lend it, has been found, dates convenient for the owner and the Society are decided on, if possible so as not to clash with other fixtures.

We are no longer so reliant on generous hosts who have the improvement of gundogs sufficiently at heart to lend their grounds free of charge and invite their guests to shoot. Trials are more often taking place on commercial shoots, some of which have many such Trials per season, not only for Spaniels and Retrievers, but also for Pointers, Setters and H.P.R.s (Hunt, Point, Retrieve breeds), which are outside the scope of this book. Date clashing has

3

become a major problem; there are now many more more trials than when the original book was written. The Kennel Club attempts to help Field Trial secretaries to avoid the worst clashes, but as the demand for Trials is so high, and the season is so short (particularly for Retriever Open Stakes), some clashes are inevitable.

Three judges have next to be appointed, and their promise to officiate obtained. Probably the fairest way of selecting judges is for each member of the Committee to select and write down six names. The Secretary will then issue invitations to judge to those obtaining most votes, until three accept.

Alington's suggestions concerning the selection of judges are very sound. Nowadays names are often suggested by one person, only to be vetoed by another, and the harassed Field Trial secretary has his or her work cut out in attempting to make a list.

Many more Retriever Trials now have four judges rather than three. This is partly in order to train new judges, partly so that a dog which performs badly in its first round can be discarded (having been seen by more than one judge), thus saving game, and partly because in walked up trials the line is far easier to organise in two halves rather than in three thirds, especially when 'crossing' retrieves. There are strong arguments for retaining the three judge system in trials judged entirely on drives, if only for the reason that three dogs instead of two can be worked at once thus saving considerable time.

These preliminaries having been settled, the Schedules can be issued. The most important information they contain is the date of the Trials, the venue, the Stakes to be decided, and the order in which they are to be run, conditions of entry, amount of entry fees and the closing date for applications for nominations.

One might wish to add to this list the names of the judges.

Stakes are limited to a certain number of competitors. If applications exceed this number, a ballot becomes necessary. Those successful in the ballot, or those who subsequently accept a nomination which has become vacant, are eligible to compete in the Stake. All Societies, with the exception of the Kennel Club, give priority in the ballot to their own members. [In recent years the Kennel Club has also given priority to its own members.] Many Societies have a rule by which the order in which names come out of the ballot becomes the order on the card. If not, a draw for numbers on the card is necessary.

Nowadays the order of the draw is most frequently the order on the card and normally reserves come in at the same number as the dogs they are replacing.

Most Trials start at about 9.30 a.m. The judges decide what positions in the line they will take up. Six guns, two for each judge, are appointed, and the first six dogs on the card, with their handlers, are called for. Numbers 1 and 2 are usually taken by the judge on the right; 3 and 4 come under the judge in the centre; 5 and 6 go to the left-hand judge. When a dog's first trial is completed the dog next in order on the card, if not under a judge, is called for, and so on till every dog in the Stake has been tried once. After this judges can call up dogs for trial in any order they please.

In theory most Trials start at 9 a.m. but in practice it is usually at least 9.30 a.m. before the first shot is fired. More often than not there are still six guns, both for the three or four judge systems, with two guns to a single judge or three guns to a pair. However, it is up to the host how many guns he invites, or on a commercial shoot, it is often up to the guns themselves how they make up their team. Lowest numbers are always on the right and we talk about the 'first round' rather than the 'first trial' to avoid confusion. It is normal practice to give dogs two retrieves, or two first dog attempts, in their first round. In theory, it is still possible to call up dogs thereafter in any order, but it is never done. Numerical order is sometimes strictly adhered to right up to the end: in other cases during the run-off the order might be varied to confirm the position of the top dog or to give another the chance of taking the lead, according to how the judges are assessing the dog work. Most often, in the second round, which includes all dogs which have neither committed a cardinal fault, nor, under the four judge system, performed at below the required standard, only one retrieve

5

is given, unless there is certain to be a plentiful supply of game. Thereafter, subsequent rounds normally consist of two retrieves until the Trial reaches a conclusion.

The nature of the tests set by the judges depends largely on the ground shot over, and the game on it. There is no doubt, however, that walking turnips, bracken, or other good cover in line, helps judges to come to a decision more than any other form of shooting, and is, therefore, resorted to whenever possible.

Most Field Trial judges still consider that walking up is far and away the easiest and fairest way of conducting Trials. Less game is required because first dog down failures can be eliminated, even if the following dog(s) fail to find the game, and also because some retrieves at a driven Trial are of little value, for example the first few birds retrieved from an area of cover in which several have fallen. However, in some parts of the country, walking up is impractical. Nowadays the vast majority of walked up Trials takes place in sugar beet, or turnips if in Scotland.

During the first time down the card, it is an unwritten law that judges shall only send the dogs under them for game shot by the two guns allotted to them.

The 'unwritten law' mentioned by Alington is now covered by 4.d. in the *Kennel Club Guide to the Conduct of Field Trials*. 'If game is shot very close to a dog, which would make a retrieve of no value, the retrieve may be offered to a dog under another judge. During the first round of the Stake dogs should, whenever possible, have the opportunity to pick game shot by their own guns.'
Another part of the Guide refers to a situation when most of the game is being shot on one side of the line, and other judge(s) and their dogs are starved of game. It is recommended that all game shot by one or more of the guns on the favourable side should be offered to the judge or judges who are short.

There are other rules and regulations adopted by some Societies and not by others. None of them can be said to unduly hamper judges, who are given the free hand which is necessary to enable them to arrive at their decisions.

How Field Trials are Conducted

It is no longer true that different societies have different rules for conducting Field Trials. They all abide (or they should) by the same Kennel Club rules.

Though walking in line, and having game shot as it rises, is the fairest and most satisfactory way of testing Retrievers, driving is often resorted to, and is indeed the only possible way of killing game when cover is short. As a matter of fact, no test of a Retriever is complete until he has been seen at a drive. There have been cases in the past, and no doubt will be in the future, of dogs which whine and even bark at a drive, but remain quiet when walking in line. The temptation to run in is also greater to some dogs during a drive.

What Alington says about testing Retrievers at drives is still spot on. In fact today it is impossible to make up a F.T.Ch. (Field Trial Champion) without a certificate, signed by two 'A' judges, that it has sat quietly at a drive.

The criticism is often made that Field Trials are entirely different to a day's shooting, but those who would belittle them on this ground must remember that on a day's shooting the main object is to shoot and collect the game. At a Trial we are out with the sole object of testing the dogs. Some of the guns, particularly those who accept an invitation to shoot at Trials for the first time, seem to become nervous and certainly shoot below their real form. It may be that they are under the impression that all eyes are upon them, and that their reputations are at stake. The fact is that everyone is so interested in the work of the dogs that the work of the shooters, at any rate as individuals, is seldom noticed. The guns can, however, be of great assistance to judges if instead of killing birds at the easiest angle, they will kill them so that they fall where a test for a dog is provided. It is a great mistake to imagine that moderate shooters supply the best tests at Trials. They should all be good shots; if possible equally good.

Alington's remarks about guns are tactful but he hits the nail on the head when he says that all the guns should be good shots and,

7

if possible, equally good. Advice to guns from judges today often contains the words 'Just get 'em on the ground'. In other words, no clever tricks like deliberately trying to shoot runners.

Field Trials are not open to the public as spectators, but anyone really interested in dog work is not likely to find much difficulty in getting permission from the owner of the ground to see them. Spectators are not allowed in the line, but must follow a guide, who is usually provided with a red flag. The contour of the land will determine the view to be obtained of the proceedings. Numbers fixed to the arms of their handlers denote the dogs as numbered on the card, and large numbers corresponding with these are hoisted on a board for all to see when a dog is sent out to retrieve.

Probably it is acceptable these days for would-be spectators to contact the Field Trial secretary rather than the host. He or she will be aware of how the latter feels about spectators, but normally they are welcome and indeed can be useful as volunteer beaters, markers etc.

There are of necessity points where Spaniel Trials differ from Trials for Retrievers. Stakes are provided for single Spaniels, Braces and Teams – a team being three or more. Never more than two handlers are down at the same time, consequently, two judges only are required. A referee is also appointed, who can be called in to decide if the two judges fail to agree. The card is run through once as in Retriever Trials. Number 1 competing against 2; 3 against 4; and so on. Instead of retrieving only, a Spaniel has to act as beater as well, and the manner in which he finds and pushes out game to be shot is, or should be, considered of greater importance than the perfection of his retrieving. While Retrievers have to wait for their opportunity, Spaniels are demonstrating their abilities the whole time they are under the judges; consequently, many more Spaniels can be judged in a day than Retrievers. As many as two sixteen dog Stakes have been finished in the day. In the writer's opinion it is impossible to come to satisfactory

8

decisions when thirty-two Spaniels have to be judged in one day. A few years ago the average standard of breaking and ability was nothing like so high as it is today, and what was possible in the way of judging then, is impossible at the present time. The number of guns shooting at Spaniel Trials varies, but three can well cover the ground to be worked by two single Spaniels. Having found and pushed out the game, a Spaniel is expected to retrieve it on command.

Stakes are no longer provided for Spaniels working in braces or teams. There are still only two judges but the role of the referee has been dispensed with, mainly because it was difficult to find a suitably qualified person prepared to watch the work, all day possibly, without being consulted at all. Increasingly a beginner judge, or even a spectator, was roped in as referee and on occasion disagreed with panel judges, to their annoyance. It is rather misleading to say that No. 1 is judged against No. 2, and so on. Each judge gives the dogs under him the length of run he considers appropriate, and one judge may easily get well ahead of the other. Almost always the senior judge goes on the right and takes the odd numbers. Nowadays it would be unheard of to try and judge two sixteen-dog Stakes in one day. Presumably standards have continued to rise since Alington was writing. It is usual to have four guns, two to each judge. If there are more than four guns the distance between the competing dogs becomes too great and game that has been flushed by neither dog may get up between them.

Trials are occasionally held for Spaniels acting as Retrievers only, but winners of them as such are not eligible to compete in the Spaniel Championship. Though Trials of this kind are rightly not considered *bona fide* Spaniel Trials, they are interesting and useful to those who use Spaniels purely as Retrievers.

It is interesting to learn that Trials used to be held for Spaniels acting only as Retrievers. All retrieving gundogs (i.e. Retrievers, Spaniels and the Hunt, Point, Retrieve breeds) used to be allowed to compete together, as Retrievers, in Trials held by the various branches of the Utility Gundog Society. However, the Kennel Club never fully recognised these 'fun' trials, so to the regret of many, they have ceased.

9

This short summary of the mode of procedure at Field Trials may well be brought to a close by one piece of advice to any dog lover who proposes to become a spectator for the first time. If such a man comes to the conclusion that he has a far better dog at home than any he has seen as the Trials, let him enter it and run it by all means; but he will do well to remember that Trials are not quite what they seem, and that his marvel at home may not reproduce his form in public.

Alington's final paragraph is as good advice to critical spectators as ever it was, except that nowadays it is far harder to obtain nominations to run in Trials, as demand for places is so much greater.

Chapter 2
Equity in Judging

The writer, who has himself judged and been judged for many years at Field Trials, will now try to provide food for thought for those about to judge for the first time, and possibly to write something which judges and judged with greater experience than himself, may find of interest. An effort will be made to show what in the writer's opinion is a fair way of dealing with some of the problems which arise at Trials, and what may be unfair. If some unfairness occasionally shows itself the writer believes it to be unintentional and due to the fact that many of the questions which crop up for decision have not been looked at from all points of view. The need for strict fairness on the part of judges is emphasised by the fact that one seldom, if ever, hears a serious grumble from a competitor who is able to attribute his dog's lack of success to bad luck. It is only when a real or fancied unfairness on the part of a judge is discovered, that nasty things are thought and often said. Luck must always largely affect the awards at Trials, and against certain forms of bad luck the best dog in the world cannot win. Luck, however, shows itself in such a number of ways that in the long run it probably evens itself out, and no dog, if it competes often enough, will be deprived by misfortune alone of his chance to win eventually. Judges cannot eliminate luck, nor would it be for the good of the Field Trial movement if they could, but they can show strict impartiality.

When Alington was writing most, if not all, judges came from the 'gentleman' class or from gamekeepers. Therefore honesty was almost always the rule. Nowadays things have changed and although

I have never as a judge observed other judges trying to 'swing' something in favour of a friend, I have seen it as a spectator on several occasions. Although he points out that luck evens itself out if the dog runs often enough, these days it is not always possible for a dog to get sufficient runs for this to happen.

All competitors have paid the same entry fee, and all are entitled to impartial and unbiased treatment whether they are novices or old hands at the game. In the first place it is necessary for those who act in a judicial capacity to completely banish from their minds everything they may know or suspect, either from previous personal observation or hearsay, about the dogs they are to judge and their handlers. They should, in fact, act as perforce does a judge of onions at a local flower show. This appears to be a comparatively easy frame of mind to put oneself into, but it is by no means so easy as those who have never tried it might suppose. The writer could mention many instances where knowledge gained from observation of a dog's work on a previous occasion has been used by a judge in order to induce it to disclose a fault which might not otherwise have been discovered. Thus, though it may be common knowledge that a certain dog has bitten live birds on some former occasion, a judge is not justified in going out of his way to find a live bird for him to retrieve during the Trial he is then judging. Against this contention it has been argued that judges are out to find the best dog, and that a fault, if there is one, should be penalised, however discovered. This argument will not hold water. Prizes are not offered for the best dogs, but for the dogs which do the best work in each Stake, and the writer holds that judges are not entitled to take into consideration, or use any knowledge but that gained during the Stake they are judging.

Alington is right to point out that judges should not use knowledge gained on previous occasions to expose faults they know certain dogs possess. However, it is to my mind perfectly legitimate, in fact desirable, if a runner has been retrieved in a dubious state during *that Trial* to try to engineer that the same dog is tried on

12

another runner. This is fairer than putting it out on the evidence of one doubtful bird.

During the first time down the card, or before anything is known of the competitors, it is necessary, if fairness is to be strictly observed, that the luck of the draw, not the discretion of the judge, shall decide:

1. The position of the dog in the line;
2. Which dog is to have the first bird;
3. The dog which is to be sent third to find a bird which two have failed on.

At most Trials nowadays there is a regulation to the effect that the lowest number on the card shall be placed on the right of the judge, but when there is no such regulation in existence, it may be as well to point out that the experienced handler is likely to take up the position he prefers, and that there is often considerable advantage to be obtained thereby, either on account of the wind, a better view of the proceedings, or because one gun shoots better than another. Some judges have been known to be deaf in one ear, and the advantage of being on the deaf side may be great.

This passage is largely irrelevant as nowadays the rule is always to have the lowest number on the right, both in the entire line (in the first round) and with each individual judge or pair of judges. However, it is still up to the intelligent competitor to position him or herself to best advantage, either where it is possible to mark or where it is easier to walk. On one occasion when we were walking through brambles, a kind judge offered to let me walk on the path. I refused his offer because my very hot bitch was less likely to run in with brambles wrapped round her neck and from a position where she did not have quite such a clear view. One of the stewards at the Trial, who knew the bitch a lot better than the judge in question, could barely conceal her mirth.

A judge should also decide beforehand which dog is to have the first bird. This may seem a small point, but if the first bird happens to be one of the few runners shot during the Stake, it may give a dog such a chance to distinguish himself that the ultimate awards are greatly influenced by his performance.

This could cut both ways, should the 'favoured' dog fail on the runner.

Again, during the first time down the card if two dogs fail and it is considered desirable to send a third dog, it is only fair that the luck of the draw should decide which dog shall attempt to wipe the eye of the other two. Failure in such a case is seldom penalised, but success may help greatly towards a high place on the award list. The writer was present at a Trial some years ago in which two dogs failed on a dead bird during the first drive of the day. Although there were four other dogs in the line, which had had no work to do, the judge sent for a dog well known for its excellence, which was not even next in order, to be tried. This dog found the bird, and ultimately won the Stake. In this case the judge was not only using knowledge which he had no right to use, but was also treating with unfairness other dogs in the Stake. It was no doubt done on the spur of the moment without thought, but caused a good deal of heartburning at the time.

The incident described above could never happen now. However, it is highly relevant to one's success in a Trial, which dogs are adjacent. The less competent they are, the better one's own chance of eyewipes. Alington refers to trying 'a third dog'. Dogs are, or should be, tried in pairs, but of course if the third dog down picks the bird, there is no opportunity for a fourth dog to make an attempt. Sometimes, if it is the three-judge system and there are six dogs in line, all six may be tried. However, judges who do this run a risk of losing six dogs out of the Stake and ending up without any prize-winners. The late Bob Baldwin told me at the beginning of my judging career, 'If you try one dog, you must try two. If you try three, you must try four.' Several instances that remain in my mind of unfair treatment were the direct result of judges, for whatever good reasons of their own, ignoring this protocol.

It is also important that every dog in a Stake should come under a judge once, before any are called up a second time.

14

If this rule is adhered to, conditions of scent, weather, ground etc. for each dog are determined by the luck of the draw for places on the card.

After all the dogs have been out once the judges have something to go on from personal observation, and it would be the greatest mistake to hamper them by regulations in any way, except with regard to the question of hard mouth, about which something will be written later.

Here it may be pointed out to those who have not judged before that the sooner judges can see all the dogs on the card once, the more equal are the scenting conditions likely to be, and the longer will be the time left at the end of the day for a thorough trial of the dogs which have done best.

It may be that voluminous notes taken about each performance are a help to some judges. If they are necessary, the writer would suggest that they be cut as short as possible, and would strongly advise the novice not to start writing until the performance he intends to describe is finished.

Notes taken by modern judges vary enormously. They are often to be seen writing in their books before the dog has delivered, thus failing to observe a poor delivery. Much time is wasted when they get together to compare notes, if one judge insists on giving a blow-by-blow description of everything the dogs under him have done. All one needs to know at the stage of the sort-out which usually follows the second round, is what grades the other judges have given the dogs they have seen. Therefore it is important that judges are trained, or learn through experience, to grade dogs in a reasonably similar manner. It is only later, when dogs appear to be lying equal, that judges have to go back through their books and try to compare performances in more detail.

Hitherto the writer has had in his mind the judging of Retriever Trials, though much of what has been written is also applicable to Spaniel judging, and the same may be said of what is to follow.

There is some diversity of practice among Retriever judges as to the licence that should be allowed to a handler in assisting his dog. Some consider that the wisest policy is to allow the handler complete liberty and to penalize him if

15

he exceeds certain undefined limits. The uncertainty of these limits is one of the grave objections to this policy. Judges themselves look upon the matter in different lights. The consequence is that handlers, particularly novices, are apt to become nervous and afraid to move when there could be no objection to their doing so. In this way the chances of a good dog may be ruined. Again, if handlers are allowed to go where they please, a number of birds are wasted from a judge's point of view. Some handlers do so much themselves that it is impossible to tell what the dog could have done without his handler's pedestrian assistance. Time is all too short for coming to any satisfactory decision at Trials and birds often none too plentiful. Judges should, therefore, make the most of every bird killed. As an instance, take the case of a bird which falls, let us say, over a fence. The judge, having dogs Numbers 1 and 2 under him, sends No.1 for the bird. The handler of No. 1, finding that he cannot get his dog over the fence, and knowing that his movements will be unrestricted, takes his dog over the fence with him, works him from the other side, and the dog is successful. Here is a completely wasted bird, and one which might have provided valuable information and the opportunity to compare the merits of Numbers 1 and 2.

This would never happen these days. Judges almost always say, 'Try from here'; or 'You can move so that you can see your dog'; or 'Don't go further forward than my stick' (stuck in the ground). Some handlers are notorious for creeping forward but few are likely to get over a fence without permission.

The writer is convinced that the most satisfactory method of treating handlers is for judges to inform them before the Trials commence that they will not be penalised for going where they please, unless they fail to stop when ordered to do so by a judge. If this practice is adopted, and we revert to the instance of the bird over the hedge, the handler of No. 1 having failed to get his dog over the hedge and being prevented by the judge from going himself, No. 2 is sent. One of three things may now happen. No. 2

16

may refuse to go over the hedge; he may go over and fail to find the bird; or he may go over and wipe the eye of No. 1. If No. 2 also refuses to go over the hedge and the judge decides to allow either Nos. 1 or 2 to get the bird without calling up a third dog, it is obviously only fair to give the handler of No. 1 the first chance of getting over the fence. At the worst the judge has at least learnt that neither dog can be sent over that fence – knowledge which could not have been obtained without restricting the movements of the handlers.

But another difficulty arises when handlers are allowed free liberty of movement. As an illustration, let us suppose that a snipe is lying dead on the far side of a strip of bog forty yards wide, and that the same judge who places no restrictions on handlers, having changed to Numbers 7 and 8 dogs, sends No. 7 for the snipe. His handler, partly because he doesn't want to get wet, and partly because he wishes to show his dog off to the best advantage, remains on the near side of the bog, gets his dog almost to the other side by signal, but fails to gather the bird. The handler of No. 8, knowing that his dog will not cross the bog unaided, plunges in to the knees, followed by his dog, which he works from three quarters of the way across, and gets the snipe. Here is a case of a gallant failure, against an ignominious success, and it would be interesting to hear from one of those judges who believe in allowing handlers complete liberty of movement, which of the two performances he would give preference to.

Again, this would not happen nowadays but the point is interesting.

Novice judges often find difficulty in deciding what length of time they shall give a dog in which to find a bird before calling him up, and one does at times hear grumblings from a handler that so-and-so was given far longer in which to find a bird than he had been, and was thus given an unfair advantage. To lay down a hard and fast rule on the subject would be impossible. The time given must depend on the way the dog is working. A dog which is hunting with intelligence, obviously trying, without disturbing unnecessary ground, can safely be given a longer time in which to find the bird than the wild or slack hunting animal. Speaking generally, it is the writer's experience that too much time is apt to be given for the recovery of birds which are known to be runners. Dogs which have evidently no chance of finding the bird except by a fluke, dogs which pass over the fall and the line time after time without owning it, are often kept down so long that there is little or no chance for a second dog. Judges themselves know well that the first dog should often be called up earlier, but allow him to continue his obviously futile efforts from an excessive desire to be fair. Excessive, because this practice only results in unfairness to the second dog.

My own rule of thumb, when judging, on a bird thought to be dead, is to call the dog up at the point where finding the bird would do the dog no good; that is, to class it as a 'B' retrieve. On a runner, I go along entirely with Alington. However, I have noticed a tendency for modern judges to give second and subsequent dogs less time than the first. This must be wrong, especially if they themselves are then going to go and look for the bird. All too often competitors are told, 'Just send your dog for a quick look, but we don't think the bird is there.' When, after a quick look, the dog has failed, and the judges, after a thorough and detailed search have themselves found the game, all dogs which have been tried on that bird have to be eliminated, regardless of how much or how little time they have been given.

The question of what a handler should be allowed to do in the case of a bird which is known to be a runner often arises. This must be decided by each individual judge for himself, but the writer's own opinion is that if the dog has obviously seen the fall and goes straight to it, it is only in very exceptional circumstances that the handler of the first dog should be allowed to go forward to render assistance. If he fails, the handler of the second dog should be allowed to put his dog right on the fall or line. If, however, the first dog sent has not marked the fall, and starts off anywhere but in the right direction, the writer would allow the handler to take his dog to the fall.

This is a case where the vast improvement in training and handling makes the above observation obsolete. The second dog, if it has either not marked or has forgotten the mark, should be capable of being handled onto the fall. However, it always used to be the practice to take the second and subsequent dogs nearer the fall than the first dog sent. Personally I think it it is a pity that nowadays this is hardly ever done. In fact many present day judges move all but the first dog off their mark, in the interests of making it the same retrieve for all. This is something with which I strongly disagree. Dogs should be allowed to remember their mark, and good ones do, even when third or fourth dog down.

Many experienced judges may disagree with the opinion above expressed, but it must be borne in mind that it applies only to the case of a bird which is known to have run. It may be argued that if a dog has had the chance to mark the fall he ought to have done so, but marking at Trials is very different to marking at an ordinary day's shooting, and perhaps due allowance is not always made for this fact. In the first place the line is nearly always congested and the chance of someone obstructing the dog's view is very great. Again, a dog which has been watching his master shooting for months suddenly has to fix his attention in other directions at Trials. There are also many distractions at Trials which make marking to some extent a matter of luck. A dog may have marked one bird and been sent for another. In runner-getting, the fall is all important, and the dog which owns the fall and follows the line from it, gives a far more impressive performance than the one which picks up a line which happens to be the right one, some distance from the fall, and then finds the bird. Hence the contention that in certain circumstances a handler should be allowed to make certain that his dog has a chance to own the fall.

Times have changed. Most current Field Trial dogs do not spend the rest of their time being shot over by their owners. Contrary to popular belief, the vast majority, though unfortunately not all, work on shoots picking up, or beating in the case of Spaniels, otherwise how would they acquire sufficient experience? Therefore Retrievers walking in line in Trials are probably more used to marking under such circumstances than when Alington was writing. However, he is perfectly correct in stating that dogs are often unable to mark because someone is in the way.

Chapter 3
Hard Mouths

O ne of the most difficult, perhaps the most difficult,
points judges have to decide is whether or not
a dog has bitten game so badly as to merit its
elimination from the Stake. The writer himself has made a
special study of 'hard mouth', has opened hundreds of
rabbits and hares, and made careful examination of endless
birds, yet after thirty-six years he freely confesses that there
are many cases of game being retrieved, badly damaged,
apparently by the dog, where he is too uncertain to be able
conscientiously to bring in a verdict of guilty. It may be
said at once for the benefit of those who may not have stud-
ied this subject very closely that it is absolutely useless,
when examining game for damage to trust to eyesight; in
fact, in nine hundred and ninety-nine cases out of a thou-
sand any damage which can be detected by the eye is
evidence that the dog is not hard in the mouth. Such
damage as is done by the hard-mouthed animal can only be
detected by touch. Where birds are concerned the crushing
of the back or ribs, or both, are the usual signs and most
easily detected; in ground game, unless opened, the ribs,
which can be easily examined by the fingers, are the only
indication of damage, not necessarily by the dog, to be
found.

Everyone who judges or intends to judge, though they
need not be experts in anatomy, should know what all
undamaged game feels like. Many would probably be
surprised to find the difference for instance between the
ribs and back of a young immature pheasant and of an old
one. Before deciding what has caused the damage, it is

important to be able to be certain that there is damage. The actions of a hard-mouthed dog often give rise to suspicion before the bird arrives in the judge's hands; but some of these actions are also the actions of the ultra soft-mouthed dog, so that as a rule nothing more than suspicion should be aroused by them.

A judge should be particularly careful in his examination of game retrieved by dogs which take a long time picking up, which deliberately put the bird on the ground once, perhaps several times, on the way back. Game which slips out of a dog's mouth, obviously owing to a very light hold, is another matter. Dogs which seem to have a very tight hold when delivering, and a reluctance to give the game up, should also be watched. Some dogs also catch strong runners in a suspicious way, rather as a terrier does a rat. Even if all these suspicious circumstances are in evidence, and the game is also damaged, there may be other factors in the case exonerating the dog from blame. All judges are liable to make mistakes, and though some dogs have undoubtedly been wrongly penalised for biting game, it is probable that more have escaped the penalty which they deserved.

The following instance, which actually happened at a Trials, will show how careful a judge must be before coming to any definite conclusion. A bird with some life in it fell over a thick belt of trees. Unseen by any but two spectators, a collie ran up, bit the bird several times and returned to his master, who was working in the field, leaving the bird where he found it. One of the competitors, after a long hunt, eventually gathered this bird and paid the full penalty for being hard in the mouth. Another case in point happened to the writer, who shot a pigeon one evening as it was getting dusk. The bird fell in a small close covered with long grass, and the dog sent to retrieve it was one with which the owner had had several differences of opinion with regard to tenderness of mouth. When delivered the pigeon had a hole in its breast, which, as it apparently fell on grass, could only have been caused by the dog's tooth.

At any rate that dog got the blame, and took the consequences.

The foregoing is such an excellent description of the diagnosis of hard mouth and consequent measures to be taken by a fair judge, that this is the first place in the chapter where I feel comment is needed. But I wonder how he showed his displeasure with the dog for having apparently bitten the bird, and what good he thought would come of his actions?

The following morning the owner happened to walk across the grass close where the previous evening the pigeon had fallen; in the centre of it stood a very small young apple tree which had been recently pruned. The feathers where the pigeon had fallen were plainly to be seen close to this tree. Further examination of the tree showed a feather and some congealed blood on one of the small spikes left after pruning. The writer, realising that he had unjustly blamed the dog, returned to the kennels, let him out, and gave him as enjoyable a morning as he could by way of reparation. This happened many years ago, and, owing to the lesson learned from it, the writer has never since failed to examine the fall where any possibility of doubt could exist.

Though these two cases are unusual, somewhat similar ones are of almost daily occurrence, and only show the necessity for a thorough investigation before finally condemning for hard mouth. Dogs have on more than one occasion been knocked out for delivering a bird alive, but in a scratched and lacerated condition. A bird in this state is the clearest possible evidence in favour of the dog and of a soft mouth. The lacerations are in fact almost invariably caused by the hold being so light as to allow the teeth to slip. A strong running pheasant, or a bird which has got wedged into a difficult place, is apt to be treated in this way. When a case of this kind arises, and the judge is in any doubt, he should in common fairness find and examine the spot from which the bird was retrieved.

Students of current Field Trial regulations and advice to judges, will recognise in the section on hard mouth, 'A bird in this state is the clearest possible evidence in favour of the dog and of a soft mouth.'

There are those who argue that provided the judges are reasonably certain that a dog has bitten game once, he should not be given another chance. Their argument, which is very sound, is that there are some dogs which are in the habit of biting an occasional bird only, and that they might not commit the offence again during the Trial. It is also probably true that there are more cases of hard mouth which escape penalization than there are of soft ones which mistakenly incur it. Unless certain beyond the possibility of doubt, the writer himself prefers to see the offence committed twice, i.e. to give the dog a second bite. It is a very serious offence, the habit is in some cases hereditary, and the value of a dog found guilty of it is enormously reduced for stud purposes. Judges without vast experience often officiate, and it is seldom that even the expert is justified in voting for the extreme penalty for a first offence unless proved beyond doubt. If the question of hard mouth has been dwelt on unduly, it is to be hoped that at least some of the difficulties confronting judges with regard to it have been shown.

I am not aware of what, if any, rules about hard mouth were in place in 1929. Now, the rule is that the damaged game has to be shown to the handler and all the judges, but this is not often done. The usual reason given for not doing so is that it would be embarrassing for the handler if the Trial were to be stopped so that a judge could carry the damaged game up the line to show to the other judges.

What I and most other judges do is to show the game to the handler and ask a steward to keep the bird on one side until there is an opportunity to show it to at least one other judge. If he is in no doubt, the dog goes. If there is doubt, the other judges are also consulted and possibly the dog gets a second chance. There is no perfect way of dealing with hard mouth as it is very much a matter of opinion. A bird can be in on one side, caused by the shot. I have

24

picked up by hand plenty of flat birds. It has to be borne in mind, however, that birds picked up by hand have usually been shot rather close.

The worst possible scenario is that which once happened to me. I was competing with a not very brilliant bitch in a two day Open Stake. She was running the Trial of her life. After a drive on the second day there were nine birds down, and she was sent, obviously after considerable delay, for the ninth, which she failed to find. No other dog was tried behind her, and the judges did not look for the bird, but my bitch was not called for again. When I met one of the judges on a subsequent occasion, I asked him what the problem had been and he replied 'I think there was a query about her mouth'. Maybe his recollection was wrong. I hope so.

I greatly admire the strength of mind of a (at the time) 'B' judge, who stood up to a very well known landowner when a dog she was judging returned across a river with half a pheasant. The host said, 'No-one would be allowed to pick up here if his dog brought back birds like that.' It was obvious that the dog had had to pull the bird out of a rabbit hole or other constricted space, and it was agreed by the judges that the dog should be forgiven.

A similar thing happened to me once on a shoot, when the owner of the estate called me across just as a bitch of mine hunting in cover came out with half a pheasant. I was terrified that another dog of mine hunting the same cover would come out with the other half. I quickly passed the half bird to a local farmer, with the hissed request 'Can you get rid of that for me?' He did. I can only assume that my bitch had had to pull the bird down from out of a tree fork.

There have been judges, past and a few present, who were notorious for putting dogs out for hard mouth on very little evidence. To be judged by one of them was one of the many pieces of bad luck which come under the general heading of 'the luck of the draw'. It is so difficult nowadays to get into Trials (Retriever Trials even more so than Spaniel Trials) that picking and choosing judges is hardly an option.

Once, when I was running a Spaniel, the judge queried a torn bird that had fallen into cut off rows of spiky thorn, a classic case of damage caused by where the bird fell. The judge queried my bitch's mouth but I am afraid I was sufficiently unsporting as to request a second chance. Finally a bird was shot, a long way out in some cover where the bitch could only get a general idea of where it had fallen. She made a brilliant job of the retrieve. In fact that little Spaniel was as good a retriever as any Labrador I have ever had. The judge's comment was, 'Oh, well, she'll only ever be a CoM (Certificate of Merit) dog.' I think she proved him wrong over the next few years by winning two Utility and two Spaniel Trials, plus numerous other awards.

Chapter 4

Retrieving and Delivery

L et us now pass on to the pick up, return and delivery
of Retrievers, the same remarks being equally applicable to Spaniels.

I would dispute this. These days a lower standard of delivery is
acceptable from Spaniels, on the grounds that they are likely to
have had a hard hunt through cover immediately prior to the
retrieve, and this should be allowed for. However, what is not
acceptable, even in a Spaniel, is for it to circle the handler several
times, or crawl on the ground as if afraid to approach. This would
never be acceptable with a Retriever, which is expected to present
its game in such a manner that the handler could take it with one
hand.

This is the part of the work at Trials which spectators can
as a rule see best and probably appreciate most. They find
themselves able to criticise it with intelligence and seldom
fail to do so. It is easy to see whether a dog goes out fast to
a bird he has marked, picks up almost in his stride, and
returns quickly with a perfect delivery. This is as it should
be, very spectacular and deserves credit. It is not, however,
quite such a simple matter for a judge to decide what credit
the performance deserves as it appears at first sight. Many
things may have to be taken into consideration. The pick up
is to some extent a knack either natural to the dog or taught.
No dog, however, can pick up game of any kind quickly if
lying in certain positions, provided he has a soft mouth.
There are dogs which invariably fumble badly and take a
long time to lift their game; if habitual, this is a fault which
wastes time and should go against them. On the other hand,

dogs have been severely criticised for picking up slowly when the position in which the game happened to be lying rendered a quick and tender pick up impossible. Nothing hinders a dog's pick up so much as extraneous matter, particularly if it happens to be of the briar nature and growing, which he sometimes gets into his mouth together with the game. Before penalising a dog for picking up slowly a judge should be sure that there was no excuse for it. Some habitues of Field Trials may remember the case of a Double Champion [presumably he means what we would now call a Dual Champion] which returned with a cock pheasant in his mouth, completely hidden by a large turnip, the leaves of which the dog had seized while picking up the bird. The dog's pick up was exceptionally quick so the turnip had to come as well as the bird. Had the turnip been a growing briar it would have been a different matter.

The return depends for one thing on the nature of the ground. A dog may complete his task like lightning on a grass field, but never go out of a stumbling trot on ploughed land. A fact which is often overlooked by spectators, and possibly by some judges, is that few if any dogs will come back quickly over apparently easy going ground which is in reality covered with short gorse. Certain kinds of prickly thistles, sometimes found even in turnip fields in large patches, will often stop a dog which would otherwise have come back fast. When comparing the pace at which different dogs return – and it may be that there is so little difference between them in their other work that their return becomes the deciding factor – it must be remembered that the size and weight of the game carried has to be taken into consideration. An eight pound hare is a very different proposition for a dog to one weighing five pounds. Then again, a dog which has been doing a lot of work, particularly on a hot day, and has found his game after a gruelling hunt, is greatly handicapped in his return against a competitor which is quite fresh. This applies in an even greater degree to Spaniels, which will be dealt with more fully in a later chapter.

Judges today do not use their common sense nearly enough about the above points, about which Alington is perfectly correct.

The pace of the return is to some extent governed by the kind of hold the dog has of his game. Over and over again when standing among the spectators, while a dog is retrieving, one has heard a groan and the words: 'What a pity he's dropped it'; as if this was quite sufficient to ruin the dog's chance. Judging from reports of Trials in the papers, and things one hears said, it is probable that some judges are inclined to penalise dogs for dropping their game while retrieving, pretty severely.

Some breeds tend to drop game more than others. Goldens do it more than Labradors, and whether this should be tolerated by judges on the grounds that it may mean they have more tender mouths, is a point on which every judge has to make up his or her mind. I have seen no Chesapeakes run in Trials, except abroad, but they seem to vary between droppers and rather tight holders-on. Flat-coats, in my experience, are often as good as the best Labrador, but occasionally a Flat-coat is found with a hard mouth problem.

Whether or not a penalty should be incurred for what undoubtedly causes delay and mars the finish of the performance, depends on the reason the game was dropped. If a dog invariably drops his game, even if only the size of a partridge, several times, it is a most objectionable habit. If, on the other hand, the game slips once in a while, owing to the tenderness of a dog's mouth, particularly in the case of heavy game, such as hares, it seems unwise to penalise it. Unwise, because a really tender mouth is of the utmost value and importance, and if breakers [trainers] find that the above-mentioned fault is to be heavily penalised, they will discard the softest mouthed dogs for those which take a firmer hold and never drop their game. The step from a firm hold to too firm a hold is not a long one, and in time to come we might find ourselves with a very much harder mouthed breed of dog than we have at the present time.

29

Again, it is a pity that so many modern judges do not view these matters like Alington, who is absolutely correct in all his comments about dropping game.

There are some who would like to see the retrieving of hares entirely abolished at Trials. The writer, however, agrees with those who argue that a dog is not broken [trained] unless it will retrieve a dead or wounded hare one minute, and remain absolutely steady to an unwounded one the next. It is sometimes contended that if one dog has a hare to retrieve, all should be asked to retrieve them. One might just as well argue that if one dog is sent for a snipe or woodcock, all should be given the same test, which would be impossible. This, therefore, must remain one of the many things which are decided by luck. If, however, there are enough hares for all, all should be asked to retrieve them if possible. The case of the wounded hare, strong enough to give a dog a long course before being caught, is rather different. Such a course may take a lot of steam out of one dog, while the others have no such strain to undergo, and taking all things into consideration, this must be put down as an unfair test at Trials. Judges should be particularly lenient where the pick up and return with a dead hare are concerned. The main object of asking a dog to retrieve a hare at all at Trials is to show that he is sufficiently broken to be able to be sent for a dead or wounded hare and yet remain steady to the unwounded ones.

These days, when we have to be so careful to do nothing which would appear to spectators to be cruel, if a hare is wounded the gun is always asked to shoot it again. Of course if it goes off dangling a leg this is not possible, and personally, I wish that people who cannot shoot hares dead in nine cases out of ten, would not attempt to do so. But there are several estates, known to us all, where Trials would never be finished if no hares were shot. During one I remember particularly, three pheasants and one pigeon comprised the bag, along with a great many hares. This was a Trial held in sugar beet.

A judging conundrum in which I was concerned also involved a

30

hare, thought to be dead, which had gone out of the beet and into some cover. When the first dog sent got to it, it started to squeal and the dog came away. Instead of sending another dog, the senior judge of the other pair strode into the cover, retrieved the hare himself and killed it.

When it came to discussing the incident, the other three judges all agreed that the dog which had refused to pick the wounded hare should not be penalised, on the grounds that if it had been known that the hare was not dead, the dog would not have been sent, it being a Novice Stake. My view was, and is to this day, that a dog's primary job is to pick up wounded game rather than dead game, which could often be picked up by hand, and if a mistake is made and a novice dog is sent for a wounded hare, there being no rule stating that it should not be, the dog should complete the task or be penalised.

Another incident involving a wounded hare took place at a different Trial. The first dog sent for a hare, later discovered not to be dead, refused to pick it up. In my opinion the judge concerned gave the dog far too long. It was a painful incident to witness. By the time the second dog was sent, the hare had moved on, further than we all realised. The handler blew her whistle when her dog got to where she thought was the right place, but the dog took no notice, went on another thirty yards or so and came back with it, a case of disobedience but with a good result. This was a good example of the late Daphne Purbrick's dictum, 'When in doubt, go back to what you would want on a shooting day'.

A lady who started in Trials before I did, an amateur with very few dogs, achieved considerable success. However, she ran a novice bitch many years ago which would not pick up a wounded hare. It was unusual, even in those days, to be asked to pick one up in a Novice Stake. She came up against this situation in three Trials running.

You may be sure that if your dog has a weakness, a Trial will find it out. I had something similar with a novice bitch which would not enter water from a distance. Needless to say, she was shortly on the transfer list as she was never going to be a brilliant Trial bitch.

Chapter 5

Some Tests

There are only two holds which a dog can take of a full-grown hare and lift it clear of the ground without damaging it. One is by the skin, and the other between the ribs and the spot where the hind legs join the back. Let anyone who has not tried it attempt to lift, hold and run with a large hare held by the thumb and fingers across the ribs: he will find that he cannot do so, with his palm held downwards, without breaking a rib. Even the dogs which have a gift for picking up hares sometimes get a wrong hold, and are obliged to drop them in order to get a proper grip. Much more so is the case with those which have not acquired the knack. If smartness has been shown in the pick up and return of other game, the writer himself overlooks a certain amount of fumbling with a hare. It may be well here to remind spectators and those who write criticisms of performances from a distance, that many things are visible to judges at close quarters, which are invisible to those standing some distance away.

I remember an occasion when, along with a Labrador or two, I had with me picking up on a big shoot, my very small Springer Spaniel. One of the guns remarked dismissively, 'Are they breeding them as small as ferrets now?' I took a great risk and sent my little bitch for her very first hare in full sight of this man. With no hesitation, she picked it up, balanced and carried it perfectly. It is a matter of having the instinct to know how to do it. Many will remember Paul Rawlings' 18 lb Open Stake winning black Cocker, Ormewood Penny, which also had not the slightest difficulty in carrying hares.

On the same day as Layerbrook Guinea successfully retrieved her first hare, I took an equal chance and sent Manymills Encore W.D.Ex. (Working Dog Excellent) U.D.Ex. (Utility Dog Excellent) C.D.Ex. (Companion Dog Excellent) for a large Canada goose that had been shot. She had never picked up, or even seen, a goose before but brought it back with as little difficulty as Guinea had done with the hare. It is partly a matter of courage, and Corrie (Encore) was a very brave bitch. She would hurl herself at the scale jump in Working Trials, even when not in a good position to return over it, often succeeding by sheer determination. She was also a first class tracking and searching bitch and, had I not moved to Essex in 1975 where my tracking activities virtually ceased, she might have followed her dam, W.T.Ch. (Working Trial Champion) Manymills Tanne, down that road. Corrie was born in 1973.

She was one of my all time favourites and unlucky not to be made up to F.T.Ch. She came second in her first two-day Open, having needed no whistle on her first seven retrieves, and having eyewiped two A+ dogs on her eighth. After that occasion she almost always ended up in the first five, but there was usually one slightly imperfect retrieve, or an impossible runner, to prevent her winning. In one particular Trial a judge said of the first four, 'I wish we could send you all to the Championship.'

Take the very common instance of the dog which picks a bird up so that the wings are over his eyes and obscure his view. He must either drop the bird and get a fresh hold, or come back slowly, possibly in the wrong direction. In either case the probability is that he will be blamed for a poor return by those who were not in a position to see what had happened. The same remark applies to retrieving through certain crops. One of the worst are high dense potatoes, which seem to wind themselves as tenaciously round the game in a Retriever's mouth as they do round the legs of his master. Many other cases of judging from a distance might be cited, but it would serve no good object to enumerate them.

It is often asserted that Trials should be run exactly as is an ordinary day's shooting, and that dogs should only be asked to perform as they would on such a day. With this it is impossible to agree, but it is important that dogs should not be asked to do things at Trials which could never under

33

any circumstances be useful work during a day's shooting. At Trials we are out to test the dogs in every way we can during a very limited space of time, in order to find out what assistance they are likely to be to us in filling the bag quickly, and recovering dead and wounded game, during a day's shooting. During a day's shooting most of the game is picked up by hand, and a dog is only required in order to save his master trouble, or to recover birds which cannot be gathered without him. Ground on which Field Trials are held is often not so well stocked with game that judges can afford to waste anything killed, if they are to give from twelve to fifteen dogs a fair trial in the day. When this is the case it is not only fair, but good policy for a judge to create a situation which would not otherwise have occurred.

Today this sort of situation is one of the reasons why Trials on drives are so very much more difficult, and ask much more in the way of brain power from judges than the much more straight-forward walked up Trials, and they can be difficult enough! No judge is perfect: no judge has never made a mistake. Most of us have made plenty.

The first Open Stake I ever judged was on drives and used the three judge system. I am still being told to this day that I made a mistake in not putting out Berrystead Beau, handled by the late, great Dick Male. Beau was not a F.T.Ch. at the time, in fact it was the first of the six Open Stakes that he won.

He had been sent for a bird which had come down in a wood, but popped out momentarily (the handler did not try to stop him) to pick a bird lying just outside the wood. My reaction was not to put him out, but to send him back for the original pheasant, which he promptly found. In the course of the fifteen retrieves he had in that Trial, he improved all the time. There was no doubt in any of our minds that he deserved to win. One of the other, and clearly senior, judges was the late Audrey Radclyffe, and the way she decided how the last few birds were to be used, was to me inspirational as the very best way to approach such a task. The third judge was Peter Whitehead, then secretary of the Labrador Retriever Club.

Take as an example, the case of a drive which has taken up half an hour of valuable time. At the end of it a judge may find himself with two dead birds, lying twenty yards from him, in full view of both his dogs. In a case of this kind it is often possible for a judge, by moving his dogs, to place some obstacle, such as a fence or even water, between them and the otherwise useless birds. In this way information can often be gained and time saved.

Again, when walking in line a bird is often shot which falls within a few feet of someone in the line. Instead of having it gathered by hand, the line may be advanced thirty or forty yards, and a dog sent back for it. A useful test, of some value, may thus be quite fairly created.

On the other hand, tests have been manufactured at Trials with the object of gaining information which the writer submits are to say the least of it inadvisable. There always have been and always will be grumblers and grumbling at, and after a Trial; but it must surely be the duty of a judge to avoid as far as possible giving any legitimate ground for complaint. Any judge may make a mistake; if he realises it, nothing silences criticism or promotes good feeling quicker than an admission of it.

How I agree with this. So many judges will not admit to their mistakes, which in many cases could be put right at the time. I have even heard a certain judge claim, 'I have never made a mistake'. Whilst stewarding at a Championship, I quoted this remark to the man's fellow judge. 'Well,' he replied, 'He's just made one. He's sent the wrong dog.'

We all make mistakes. No one is perfect. But let's admit to them and put them right if we can.

Judges can only do good by answering questions put to them by handlers after the Trials, provided information is genuinely sought. The aggressive handler, merely anxious to show his dissatisfaction with the awards, can be treated with contempt.

Let us return to the manufactured test, and one which in the writer's opinion cannot be justified, however short game may be. Reference is made to the practice, admittedly seldom adopted, of placing by hand game previously gathered, and asking handlers to send their dogs to retrieve it. If a competitor fails to gather game put down in this way, he has a legitimate ground for complaint, unless warned before he applied for a nomination that this method of testing his dog might be resorted to. Even so there are grave objections to the practice, and handler X is sure to complain to handler Y that Mr A. (the judge) put a cold bird into a hole for his dog to find, whereas he (handler Y) had been given a warm one placed so that any fool of a dog could find it. Unequal tests are inevitable, and so long as luck is the cause of them, are taken in good part by all, but when manufactured to such an extent that cold, lukewarm, or hot game already retrieved once, is put down, luck will not be blamed for the inequalities which must exist, and they are looked upon as matters of design.

In the thirty odd years that I have been trialling, I have only on one occasion, a considerable time ago, been aware that this was happening and I am sure it is no longer practised.

The writer has himself asked a handler to try his dog for a doubtful bird, i.e. one which may or may not be down, at the same time telling him that there would be no penalty for failing to find the bird. Other judges have done the same, with the object of seeing how the dog hunted. On mature consideration this does not seem to be quite a fair test at Trials, unless all the dogs in the Stake are subjected to it. There are dogs – the writer has owned one or two himself – on which failure has a depressing and demoralising effect. They seem to lose confidence, and their subsequent work is affected by it. If such a dog happens to be the only one in the Stake sent to hunt ground where there is nothing for him to find, he may be unfairly penalised.

It is extremely difficult to draw the line between making a genuine attempt to gather every runner, but without wasting time trying numerous dogs, and looking for a bird which is known not to be there. On the very first occasion that I judged (an old-fashioned Utility Trial) a case like this arose. We were short of game and in trying to decide between an English Springer and a Golden

36

Retriever, sent them both to hunt for a non-existent bird in the open. Naturally the Spaniel came off best, and I have since always regretted having been party to this stratagem.

A frequent cause of complaint by competitors is that the handler of the second dog, which has wiped the eye of the first, was allowed by the judge to take his dog nearer to the fall than was the handler whose dog failed. Such a complaint is unreasonable in the case of a runner, but where an undoubtedly dead bird is concerned, though it seems only fair to give the handler of the second dog some advantage, it is probably fairer to fix the same limit for both handlers.

There is rarely such a thing as an 'undoubtedly dead' bird, unless it is clearly visible. A sensible judge will probably ask the handler the position from which he would like to try his dog, either from where he marked the bird, or nearer, that is if the original dog(s) were sent from closer. In the case of a crossed retrieve, when the furthest two dogs have been tried, followed by dogs in the middle (if there are three judges) and finally those closest, I would argue that because of the time which has elapsed this is perfectly fair. Those who disagree point out that it is not the same retrieve, but in view of the lapse of time, and also the fact that just as many dogs fail short as long retrieves, I am content to adhere to what is certainly now a minority view.

If both fail, the handler of the first dog can then be given another chance from any position he pleases.

Nowadays a dog is rarely given more than one chance. If a dog has had a fair attempt, and the second dog also fails, another dog should be sent for or the game picked up by hand. There was a certain judge a long time ago, whose popularity depended more on the contents of his car boot than on his ability, who asked me and another handler to try for birds in a deep ditch. We both failed and the second handler asked if he could try again from a closer position, there being no other dogs close at hand. Permission was granted and the dog succeeded at his second attempt. I immediately asked if I could also try from the closer position, and also succeeded. Thus we had wiped both our own and each other's eyes.

It often happens that two birds are down at the same time, one of which a dog has marked; the other he has not.

37

If the birds are a considerable distance apart, valuable information may be gained by sending the dog for the game he has not marked, and if he turns readily from the game his mind is set on, hunts kindly and gathers the other, the performance should be duly credited.

Two or more birds do not normally fall at exactly the same moment while walking up, unless there is a flush of partridges or pheasants, in which case it is extremely difficult for dogs, handlers and judges to mark accurately. Judges nowadays try to allocate the retrieves, as far as possible, according to the order in which they fell.

The dog has shown that he is under control and has confidence in his handler. But when two birds fall fairly near together it is not wise or perhaps quite fair to name the bird to be gathered and penalise a dog for bringing the wrong one. The argument has been advanced that it serves no good purpose in the shooting field to require a dog to gather one bird when he has marked another. This contention does not hold water when partridge driving. Most of us have met the shooter who objects strongly to having his birds picked up by a dog belonging to another gun, and unless we have sufficient control to prevent it our dogs may become a nuisance to other people.

This is an excellent argument for being able to stop a dog and handle it onto a different bird from the one it has set its mind on.

Chapter 6

Control and Natural Ability

Having mentioned the word control, which to the mind of the writer is the Alpha and Omega of breaking, it may be as well to say something about it here in connection with judging. One often hears the expression used about a dog – 'he's over broken'. Had the words used been 'badly broken' they would have been more to the point. A dog cannot be over broken, that is to say, he cannot learn too much. However much he learns during his all too short life, he must be under complete control if he is to be of the greatest use in the shooting field, and give the most pleasure to his owner. To be under complete control, a dog should be able to be guided by his master up to any distance within hearing. Few handlers ever succeed in getting such complete control as this; fewer still try. It is a long job, and seldom nowadays at Trials is a handler given the chance of showing the finishing touches on his dog's education. Such control as the writer maintains a dog should be under, in order to be perfect in this respect, has been stigmatised as 'trick work' and useless in the shooting field. It is needless to point out to the shooting man instances where complete control may prove of the utmost value, and it is probable that those who decry it as useless would be very pleased to have a little more of it in their own dogs.

Alington is perfectly correct and, of course, today it would be a waste of time to enter a Trial with a dog incapable of taking direction.

39

A well known shooting man, celebrated for the excellence of his Retrievers (at home), once ran a dog for the first time at Trials. Birds fell over a narrow stream which his bitch had not seen fall. When asked to send her for them she refused even to wet her feet, and her owner, who said he had just refused £200 for her, seemed surprised that any judge should ask such an impossible thing of her. None of these birds were more than sixty yards away; had they been two hundred yards a well broken dog would have got them all.

It should be remembered that £200 was a great deal of money in the 1920s!

The example given above is the classic answer to those who criticise as 'circus tricks' a handler's ability to put his or her dog where he wants it. I clearly remember a gun at a syndicate shoot who watched in breathless amazement while I put one of my dogs across a river and handled it, a long way out, to where a dead bird was lying. 'Isn't that impossible?' he remarked. 'I don't know about that, it's just happened!' was the best reply I could think of at the time.

It is worth repeating that 'broken', should be replaced by 'trained' in order to make the meaning clearer. It is obvious that the standard of training and handling has improved by leaps and bounds since Alington was writing.

A school of thought seems to have sprung up during recent years and has found expression in the Press, to the effect that judges should pay more attention to natural ability and less to breaking. The idea being no doubt that our breeds of gundogs can best be improved by breeding from those possessing most natural ability. On the face of it this is a most plausible theory, but impossible to carry out in practice. Natural ability consists of the qualities a dog is born with, uninfluenced in any way by human beings. If this is so, how can any judge recognise it after a dog has had eighteen months' tuition? During that time in the hands of a good man he has had many good qualities instilled into him, his own natural ability fostered and improved, and many of the undesirable qualities, born in him, eradicated. A bad natural marker may become a good one under tuition, and a dog born hard mouthed made tender.

I am sorry to disagree with Alington, for I neither know of, nor believe there to be, a genuine cure for hard mouth. It would be a great pity from the breeding point of view if there were one, as hard mouthed dogs would then be bred from, thus perpetuating the problem. It is almost the only point on which I disagree with Alington.

Some puppies seem to be born runner getters; others only learn to find them after months of practice. No one but the breaker knows these things about his dog, and no judge on earth can decide at a Trial, even if it were to last a month, whether or not certain qualities were born in a dog or instilled into him subsequently. The only qualities exhibited at a Trial which a judge can count on as likely to have been born in a competitor are nose, pace, style and drive.

Here it appears that I am hoist with my own petard. I have been known to urge in the sporting press that more attention should be paid by judges to inborn ability, and less to the results of training. However, the situation today is totally different and dogs in general are much better trained. Even in the last thirty odd years there has been a vast improvement in training and handling.

Nose, about which more will be said later, certainly cannot be thoroughly tested at a Trial. Pace, style and drive probably can be. Now there are many dogs possessing these qualities to a marked degree so long as they are allowed to hunt on their own initiative and in any direction their fancy or instinct directs, but which lose most of their pace, style and drive directly the breaker starts to exercise control. Pace, style and drive are most attractive and necessary qualities, but worse than useless in the shooting field unless under complete control. Natural ability must include the ability to be broken [we would probably describe this quality as 'biddability'], and it is impossible for any judge to estimate the value of natural qualities of this

41

nature unless he sees them in the broken animal. Field Trials will do more for our breeds of gundogs if we raise the standard of breaking required than they will by lowering it. There are not many bad dogs born, but there are comparatively few good breakers. By raising the standard of breaking required, always provided that we do not go beyond what may be of use during an ordinary day's shooting, we shall improve the breakers we have, and demonstrate to those in embryo what is possible. Breeders will see to it that dogs capable of being broken are provided and breakers will pick them to break. It is a judge's job to judge what he actually sees and not what his imagination depicts. In fact he is there to award prizes to the dogs which he considers have put up the consistently best performances. He is not there to award prizes to those which he considers might have done best had they been better broken, in better condition or better handled.

The report of a Retriever Trial signed by three good and eminently fair minded judges has appeared in the public Press, from which the following is an extract:

'We were all of the same opinion, namely, to try and select Retrievers that the average gentleman could work himself in a day's shooting and those with the most natural working abilities . . .'

Judges, even in the last ten or twenty years, have been heard to make similar remarks, which are as unrealistic now as they were then. Judges are there to judge the dogs' performance throughout the period of the Trial, and that is all.

These judges had set themselves a task which it is here submitted was not their job, and merely amounted to guesswork. It is true that if a dog cannot be handled by his own handler he cannot be handled by anyone, be he above or below the average, without further tuition. But if he is satisfactorily handled by his own handler no one can say whether or not he can be handled by the average gentleman. It may be that an average gentleman should be provided to give demonstrations, but that is another matter.

Again, these judges were out to select the dogs with the most natural working abilities. Presumably the word natural means inborn; if so a selection on this ground must again have been based on guesswork. With the exception of pace, style, which includes drive, and to some extent nose, all of which can be fostered, improved or ruined by breaking, no one but the breaker himself can tell what working quality was or was not born in his dog. Yet three experienced judges tell us that they agreed to select dogs whose performances were due to natural working ability. Judges are, of course, entitled to give preference to any kind of work done under them at a Trial which they think best, but they are not entitled to make selections on their opinion as to how the ability to do that work was produced. No other form of competition is judged on such lines. It would be a different matter if the Trial Schedule stated that preference would be given to natural ability and to dogs which could be handled by the average man. Handlers would know what to expect, and instead of trying to put up the best performance possible, would break and work their dogs in a different manner.

It is difficult to argue with any of the above. But perhaps I should mention in my own defence that I am very much a part-time dog trainer and expect my dogs to compete having had much less time spent on their training than most of their rivals.

However, in my opinion when it comes to the choice between a dog which has performed brilliantly on a runner, and one which has picked up a bird a long way out across a river, preference should go to the former, all else being equal, which it so rarely is. It is often said that runners should take precedence over eyewipes, and also that there are eyewipes and there are eyewipes. There is an enormous difference between a dog which picks up a bird, second dog down, when the first dog has been nowhere near the fall, and one which finds, third or fourth dog down, game which other competitors, hunting the same ground, have failed to find.

The following incident, which took place at Trials some years ago, shows unfairness which was quite unintentional. A natural water test was in progress; that is to say, birds were actually driven and shot so that they fell into or over water. The water happened to be a river about one hundred yards wide. All the birds shot had fallen into the river except one, which fell far into a wood on the opposite bank. Several dogs had been tried for this bird but failed to even cross the river. When it came to the turn of the last dog to be tried his handler was asked by the judges whether he would like to try for the bird over the river, or if he preferred to have a bird thrown in to test his dog. The handler elected to try for the bird on the far bank; sent his dog over the river and up into the wood, where he found the bird and retrieved it. It was a fine example of the advantage of control. The writer happened to be standing near the judges at the time and could not help hearing one say to the other: 'I don't think anything of that: the handler of the successful dog has a river at home where he practises this.'

This was clearly a ludicrously unfair comment to make and I am sure no modern judge would make it, other than perhaps as an aside that so-and-so has super water training facilities, but it would not influence his or her judgment of the performance in any way.

The judge who made this remark had no intention of being unfair, but he undoubtedly was so. He happened to be one of the chief advocates of putting natural ability above everything else, and discounted any performance for which breaking was largely responsible. He was perfectly at liberty to hold the opinion that the work done was of little value, but it was totally unfair to take into consideration the fact that X possessed a river at home. He might almost as well have said, after a fine performance on a runner, 'I don't think much of that, I saw his handler give him a dozen like that last week.' Or the judge of the Derby might in the same way ignore the winner on the strength of his knowledge that the horse had been trained on more suitable training ground, or ridden by a more capable jockey than the other runners.

All judges have their own ideas of what is wanted in a gundog, and it is no doubt all for the good of Field Trials that

44

they are not all of one mind. The writer himself probably places a higher value on control than do most judges, and he certainly finds that the greater the measure of control he obtains over his own dogs the quicker he is able to gather dead or wounded game when shooting. More important still, unnecessary ground is not disturbed in the process.

On an ordinary day's shooting there are the birds which no one sees down but which are known to be wounded and likely to be dead in a certain direction. For these a wide ranging dog, which need not necessarily be under the best of control, is required. The remainder of the game shot can be divided into four classes. There are the birds lying out in the open visible to all, for which no dog is required. There are those which are invisible owing to the nature of the cover in which they fall. There are the runners, and lastly, the birds which fall in places inaccessible to a man but easily reached by a dog if he can be directed there. For the gathering of all this game it must be of the greatest advantage to be able to direct one's dog as near to, but downwind of the fall, as quickly as possible, if the dog has not marked the bird himself. No time is then wasted and no unnecessary ground disturbed. In most cases the spot where the bird has fallen is known to within a few yards. There is nothing so aggravating or so wasteful of time as to watch a dog hunting, perhaps in most beautiful style, in any direction but where one knows the game to be.

There is a very awkward piece of thick cover on our little home shoot, where birds frequently fall. Any dog sent to retrieve has first to cross a ditch with thick bramble both sides. Then he is faced with a fence which, owing to the thickness of the cover, is impossible to jump on the left. This inevitably draws the dog to the right. The handler is then faced with the problem of the dog being out of sight, but having to be handled to the left. This is a very difficult retrieve, and one which would sort out a lot of the very best Field Trial dogs. My dogs have the advantage of having done it before but naturally not all the birds that fall in that cover are to the left, and it is easier for the dog to turn right and hope that the bird will be found there, as has also happened on many occasions.

45

To get a dog to work, as the writer considers he ought to work, is the highest form of the dog breaker's art and by far his longest job. It is not difficult, nor does it take long, to get a dog to work, like a sheepdog, without using his nose, continually expecting and almost asking his master to show him the game. This is not what is wanted in a Retriever, though for shooting purposes the writer himself would rather own a dog broken in this way, than a dog over whose movements he had no control when out working.

Unfortunately many dogs of this sort can be seen in today's Trials.

A perfectly broken dog is one which never ceases to use his nose and quarter his ground, unless and until his master signals that he wishes to direct him elsewhere. Without undue noise he should be able to be directed anywhere within hearing. Few dogs which compete at Trials are brought to such perfection as this; fewer still get the chance of showing that they are. So much so that there is little inducement for breakers to take the necessary time and trouble required to really finish their dogs.

Today's Field Trial competitors are likely to be divided into three categories, or the best of them are. There are the hunting, game-finding dogs; there are the sheepdogs; and there are the few who successfully combine the two. Of course categories overlap, and on some occasions dogs which occupy the first or second category have won major Trials.

I shall never forget the sight of the late Tommy Yetton standing still and just watching his dog, Benjamin of Shotgate, hunting for a bird during a Labrador Club Open Stake at Welbeck in 1984. Perhaps others will remember the incident also. As one of the judges, the others being Philip White and the late Eric Baldwin, I said in my report, 'The dog placed second had not had the opportunity of a runner or an eyewipe but had delighted the judges by his beautiful hunting style. His handler moreover had sufficient confidence in him to let him get on with the job without unnecessary whistling or handling.'

46

The above remarks must not be taken to mean that the writer himself despises natural ability. It is the one thing we breakers are all looking for, and there is no doubt that occasions have arisen at Trials when natural ability rightly scored over perfect breaking.

A case of this description was witnessed by the writer, who was not judging, at a Trial held in Scotland. Two birds were down near together in a turnip field, one said to be a runner, the other apparently dead. Dog Number 1, sent for the runner, after at least fifteen minutes working every inch of the ground round the fall gathered it alive. Dog Number 2, sent for the dead bird, found the fall after casting about for some time, and went off at a great pace as if on a roaring scent. His handler, believing the bird to be dead and probably thinking his dog was on a hare, whistled and continued to whistle, but the dog took no notice whatever, put up two or three coveys of partridges and several pheasants, but never leaving the line of the partridge, returned with it from the far end of the field. This was a young dog, not really under control, and, taking everything into consideration, it was one of the most brilliant pieces of work on a runner the writer has ever seen at Field Trials. The judges placed the dog first, but had he been under proper control, he would have answered to whistle and never have got the bird. This was not a case of bad handling. Any handler under similar conditions would have acted in the same way. The writer agreed with the judges, but the circumstances were exceptional.

This seems to be a classic example of Mrs Purbrick's rule, i.e. when in doubt, go back to what you would want on a shooting day. Obviously, it is preferable for the game to be in the bag rather than lost, but the vast majority of today's judges would have put the dog out for disobedience.

Some judges are apt to make allowances for bad handling, and to come to the conclusion that what they consider is a badly handled dog would have been a wonder if handled by someone else. There does not seem to be any real justification for this view. Handling is merely the act of working a dog for game, and no one on earth can handle satisfactorily a half or badly broken dog, whereas almost anyone can handle the well broken one. Handling is in fact often blamed when breaking has been at fault. It is perfectly true that many poor performers would have been wonders had they been broken differently, but it hardly seems to be the duty of the judge to decide what might have been at a Trial.

A judge is occasionally called on to decide whether or not to penalise a dog for running in owing to an involuntary movement by his handler, and mistaken by the dog for a signal. Really hard cases of this sort have from time to time occurred at Trials, and it is not the intention of the writer to suggest to judges how they should treat them. The writer himself would treat each case on its merits. If the dog had shown no symptoms of unsteadiness before the untoward event, and if he stopped at his master's command, no notice would be taken of it. If, on the other hand, the dog got completely out of control the writer would make no allowance for the handler's involuntary signal.

Many cases of this kind have occurred at Trials, but the writer can recall two in particular which happened to dogs which seemed at the time to have winning chances. In the one case a gust of wind blew the handler's hat off as a bird fell, and the handler when stretching out his hand quickly to recover it, started his dog which retrieved the bird. In the other case the handler pointed to a bird which was towering, a hare was shot as he put out his hand, and the dog undoubtedly mistook the action for a signal to go, which he did.

The standard of steadiness has improved considerably since Alington was writing. I have had various excuses given for a dog's unsteadiness, perhaps the most imaginative being that the dog thought he heard his name, 'Tor', when I said, 'Number four'.

Under negative and unsympathetic judging difficult circumstances often develop into Catch-22 situations. During a walk up, if

48

a dog lowers its head to a rabbit between its feet and the handler says 'no', the dog is put out, as he would also have been had he picked up the rabbit.

Another difficult question which may have to be decided at Trials is whether or not judges should take official notice of a dog not in the line, but which escapes from his handler and appears in front of them during a beat, either chasing a hare or committing some other offence. If so, what should be the penalty?

It may be argued that the offending dog was not under the judges at all, that they have no business to know what dog it is, and that no notice should be taken of what is merely an accident.

On the other hand it may be contended that the culpable behaviour of the dog was due to carelessness on the part of his handler, who should have kept him on a lead. That once in the field that all dogs are under the judges, that the carelessness of the handler has resulted in interference to some extent with other competitors, and that if a dog chooses this manner of showing that he is under no control, he should be penalised. Other arguments may be used on both sides, and the more one considers the matter the more difficult the answer becomes.

Two cases in point which actually happened at Trials may be mentioned, and will be remembered by those who were present. The first case happened soon after the start of the Trials. Six dogs were in the line, and the handler of a seventh dog was told to keep his dog near at hand as he would be wanted shortly. The handler walked in the line with his dog loose. A hare was shot in front of him. His dog ran in and picked it up, and the judges decided to discard him from the Stake forthwith.

The second case occurred at the very end of the Trial. The last dog in an artificial water test was being tried. A bird was thrown a few yards into the water, but almost before it fell a dog came tearing down the bank, and, in spite of the frantic vocal efforts of his handler, sprang over the dog about to be tried, into the water, and returned with the bird to his handler. Though the judges, of whom the writer was one, had not finally decided, it is probable that this dog would have been placed first in the Stake, though there was little to choose between first and second.

Another bird was thrown in for the waiting dog, which seemed rather relieved that he had not been obliged to get the first. No sooner was the bird thrown than another dog came flying down the bank, but was stopped by the shouts of his handler when close to the water. This dog happened to be the one which the judges would probably have placed second. We were in a difficult position. The Trial was over, and our two best dogs had misbehaved at the last minute. They were certainly under the judges, as all dogs had been called for the water test, though as a matter of fact neither of them would have been tried again. Rightly or wrongly, we decided to transpose the order of placing and awarded second prize to the dog which defied his handler to the limit. Thus, the dog which stopped on the brink became the winner.

If the writer was judging alone and had to decide the same question today, he would do so in the same way, though with as much hesitation as we all three decided some years ago.

All experienced judges will probably agree that even flagrant misbehaviour by dogs not actually on trial should be ignored, unless the offence is committed where the work of those being tried may be influenced. Many judges would no doubt ignore altogether anything done by dogs awaiting their turn to be called up; if so there are certainly arguments to support their view.

This reminds me of a Trial won by the first bitch I ever ran. She had triumphed fairly decisively when we found ourselves at the far end of a field of sugar beet. The host announced that, as it was not late in the day, he and his guns would like to shoot on the way back. Not having yet learned the valuable lesson never to stick my neck out, I joined the line with my bitch off the lead. A hare got up and was pursued by both the first and second prize winners. 'What are you going to do about that?' someone asked Gordon Smith, one of the judges. 'Nothing,' he replied, perfectly correctly. 'The Trial is over.'

Chapter 7

Nose and Scent

A great deal might be written on the subject of nose. It is an interesting and important organ in a gundog, and if the writer wanders occasionally into the realms of theory and away from his subject he hopes to be excused.

What is usually spoken of as a good nose in a gundog does not necessarily mean that it possesses a particularly acute sense of smell, but it does mean that the dog's brain is receptive to the particular scents which enable him to find game. This is proved by the fact that the puppy which shows its ability time after time to wind garbage, or something to eat, from a longer distance away than his mates, often turns out to have the worst nose for game. It is probable that most dogs are born with very much the same scenting powers, but use them differently. We often find for instance that a dog has a wonderful nose for a foot scent, and very little apparently for anything else, and vice versa. The writer owned one Retriever which never showed any great nose except for a rabbit sitting in a forme. He was used a lot as a Spaniel and to see him finding rabbits anyone would have said that his scenting powers were phenomenal. A party of us once shot snipe in Ireland over an Irish Setter which had been used for three years by a professional snipe shooter, entirely for snipe. She was bought and brought over to England, but never showed that she possessed a nose at all on any other game but snipe.

This is fascinating. No one these days seems to consider the noses of dogs. It is thought that either they have good noses or

52

Competitors waiting during the first drive at the Kennel Club's 27th Retriever Trial (Puppies and Non-winners) at Cheverell's Markyate, St. Albans, Hertfordshire. (circa 1936)

ABOVE: Mrs L. Charles receiving a retrieve watched by judge Mrs Heywood-Lonsdale. (circa 1965)

RIGHT: Sir George Penny (one of the Guns) and Miss A.M. Bickerton with her Shelsey Nicky at the Western Counties and South Wales Working Retriever Society's Trial at Witbury Park, Wiltshire, in 1936.

Miss A.M. Bickerton's Shelsey Mickey retrieving at the Western Counties and South Wales Working Retriever Society's Open Trial at Lockeridge, Marlborough, Wiltshire, in 1938.

Miss A.M. Bickerton sending out Shelsey Naylor at the Labrador Retriever Club's 31st Field Trial at Charlton, Horndean, Hampshire, in 1933.

A steady line at a Midland Counties Labrador Field Trial at Thoresby Park, Nottinghamshire. (date unknown)

Susan Scales with Layerbrook Guinea and Manymills Encore W.D. Ex., U.D.Ex., C.D.Ex.,
competing in the Mixed Doubles at the Game Fair at Bowood in 1979.

Susan Scales (nearest camera) with Layerbrook Guinea at the Utility Gundog Society's 57th Cup Finals Trial at Dunley, Whitchurch, Hampshire, in 1981. Other competitors were (l. to r.) S. Seall handling Layerbrook Rowena of Trioaks (partially hidden), J. Wood, C.F. Beecroft with Firjan, and Ms P. Macrae with Treunair Lunna.

Keith Erlandson with F.T.Ch. Dinas Dewi Sele at the Spaniel Championship in 1965.

LEFT: Keith Erlandson (centre) with Breckonhill Brando, the eventual winner of the Midland Counties Field Trial Society's Open Stake at Milton Park in 1957. Other competitors were (left) R.B. Weston Webb with Meadowcourt Mistress, and (right) K. Chudley with F.T.Ch. Harpersbrook Sammy, Wilbey Tite and Bryanstone Bess.

Keith Erlandson's F.T.Ch. Speckle of Ardoon at 12 years of age, the only Spaniel of any breed to win three consecutive Spaniel Championships, 1972, 1973 and 1974.

Susan Scales (nearest camera) with F.T.Ch. Manymills Milady, 1991.

bad. The fact that they are frequently specialists in what they do, including the puppy which winds 'garbage' at great distances, is somewhat forgotten nowadays.

Game finding ability is probably partly hereditary and partly due to habit, but it may be that it is quite as much due to certain qualities in the brain as to scenting powers. Dogs bred for generations for nose alone, such as the Llewellin Setters, undoubtedly develop phenomenal scenting powers, combined with game finding ability, but such dogs among Retrievers and Spaniels are very rare. In like manner there are very few gundogs born with so little scenting power that no amount of development could make them any use for finding game. The writer believes that 90% of the dogs seen at Spaniel and Retriever Trials were given by nature much the same powers of scent. In game finding some show it more than others, and they show it in different ways. Every breaker must have noticed that dogs after reaching a certain age apparently lose some of their scenting power though they probably gain in game finding ability. It may be that a dog's nose deteriorates with age to some extent, but it is also possible that the apparent falling off is due to another cause. The older a dog gets, the more he learns to discriminate between scents; he is thus inclined with age to discard as useless to him many scents which he would readily have owned as a youngster. The young dog on the other hand shows plainly by his actions the interest he takes in every scent he comes across, and may thus get the reputation for having a better nose than, say, his father.

This is often the case when dogs of two or three years of age win Trials. However, others go on for years and we all know examples which have run successfully in four or five Championships (both Retrievers and Spaniels). To me these are the ideal dogs, which do not go 'over the top' but remain calm and biddable all their lives.

For a judge to decide rightly on the merits of twenty dogs' noses at a Trial is impossible. He may have the chance to fairly compare the noses of a few but seldom on more than one class of work. All he can do is to give his decisions in accordance with what he has seen during the running of the Stake he is judging. It is not unlikely that his judgment of nose will be revised in a subsequent Stake.

This discourse on the fascinating subject of scent is probably as true today as when it was written. One of the skills required today, as it probably was in Alington's time, is the ability to decide how many dogs to try on a bird whether it be dead or a runner. Much time can be wasted looking for birds long gone, but on the other hand the Trial can be moved forward considerably by successful eyewipes. I once had the immense satisfaction, in a Utility Trial, of wiping the eyes of all other five dogs remaining in the Stake, on a dead partridge, with my small Spaniel. The bird was known to be there and it was just a matter of finding it. Whether Guinea had a better nose than the Labradors with which she was competing, who can say? Probably not, but she had a different and more effective hunting technique.

These days many dogs are assisted by their handlers to find game and they hardly seem to hunt at all, covering an area according to instructions but apparently without using their noses. Dogs like this do find game, but on bad scenting days they are likely to be beaten by the 'game finding' dogs. As has been pointed out before, the top current trainers have dogs capable of being handled accurately, and using their noses and initiative when they are in the right area. Most of us humbler folk fall between the two stools and our dogs are either too disciplined or not trained well enough.

The writer has at the moment ten Labradors and five Spaniels in his kennel: most of these he has watched at work for months, some for years, yet he would not now back his opinion on the respective merits of these dogs' noses. Most breakers would probably say the same. The number of factors, some unknown, to be taken into consideration when trying to estimate qualities of nose are so innumerable that the task is quite impossible during a short Trial, and by no means conclusive after tests, lasting for months. So little is known of scent itself that all our calculations are liable to be upset by its vagaries. We know that scent may vary greatly from bird to bird, from minute to minute, from locality to locality, from crop to crop, and from soil to soil. These variations are often inexplicable nor can anyone foresee when they will occur. There are conditions however under which scent is almost certain to be bad, and a handler may pray fervently that his dog will not be tried in a crop of mustard, nor when the sun has just melted the hoar frost, and it is hanging in drops on the grasses. Scent is almost certain to be good between 3.30 and 4.30 p.m., after a warm October day, when the thermometer suddenly drops to near freezing point. Under no other conditions would the writer care to back his opinion that scent will be good.

Let us turn from such an uncertain factor in the recovery of game as scent is, to some of those factors which are more constant though perhaps not usually recognised. Everyone will agree that some stone dead birds can be winded at a greater distance than others when lying on similar ground, and in apparently similar conditions, by the same dog. This is often due to the angle at which the bird is lying. If the wind is blowing against the lie of the feathers a far stronger scent will be given off than would be the case if blowing in the opposite direction. There is also more scent to a bird lying on its back than there is to one lying on its breast. The dead bird which can be winded from the greatest distance is one lying, if anything slightly above ground level, on its back with the wind blowing up the feathers. The dead bird which gives off least scent is one lying on its breast in a hollow and with the wind blowing with the lie of the feathers. A dog may wind the first of these birds from almost any distance, but may tread on the second and not find it. Dead birds fall in all sorts of places which affect scent to such an extent that those who take no great interest in the subject would hardly credit it. A distance of half an inch one side or other of a turnip may make an enormous difference in the scent which comes to the dog. Anyone accustomed to stalking will understand why this is so. If it is remembered that wind is affected by obstacles in the same way that water is diverted by boulders in a stream, an owner will often be able to understand the otherwise incomprehensible failure of his dog to wind game. It goes without saying that the longer a bird has been killed the less scent there is to it, and the penalty for failing to find cold game should not be heavy. Judges cannot take all the causes which affect scent into consideration at a Field Trial, and success must in most cases score above failure.

I am afraid that many of today's judges fail to take into account the time a bird has been down; whether it was shot during a drive or walking up, when there have been several birds to try for.

The subject is being dealt with at such length in order to show that a dog with a good nose may get the reputation for having a bad one during the short time he is working at a Field Trial, if luck happens to be against him. Though dead game varies greatly in scent according to conditions, the difference in the scent of live game under apparently similar conditions is at times greater. Most dog owners will agree that the bird most frequently lost is the runner which does not run. That is to say, the winged bird which squats within a few yards of where it falls, low to the ground with feathers held tight to its body. A bird behaving in this way gives off as little scent as does the partridge for nineteen out of the twenty-one days of sitting on her eggs. So long as the crouching bird remains motionless, the best nosed dog or fox in the world may pass within inches without winding it. If, however, the bird rises a fraction of an inch scent is emitted at once.

The writer happened to be standing as a spectator near one of the guns at a Field Trial, who during a drive winged a partridge which fell on an almost bare bank at the bottom of the fence in front of him, and not ten yards away. The bird crouched at once and lay there. After the drive was over, the judges brought up four dogs which they had evidently not been able to place, and sent them in turn for the bird which was still plainly visible. The first three dogs failed, though going within two feet of the bird and down wind of it, but after the third dog had passed, it moved very slightly, evidently thinking its discovery was inevitable.

The consequence was that the fourth dog wiped the eye of the other three and winded the bird immediately from some distance away. The judges, quite rightly, gave due credit for this success over failure and may have considered that the fourth dog showed superior nose to the others. Of this, however, there was no proof, and the incident is related merely to show how difficult it is to compare the scenting ability of several dogs.

The bird need not actually have moved. I can remember numerous instances of third or fourth dog down eyewipes when the conditions were the same for all the dogs. A dog of mine, Manymills Drake C.D.Ex., had done well enough on the first day of a two day Stake to be given the chance, third dog down, of a partridge lying in full view in a gateway. The host said, 'For God's sake, someone pick up that bird then we can all go home.' The dog did it with little difficulty, being a hunting dog rather than one of those which rushes here and there without using its nose.

But so many of today's judges are negative rather than positive. They are looking for reasons to put dogs out rather than keep them in. Given time the majority of Trials judge themselves. How much better for everyone to go home thinking they have been given a fair chance, rather than to have been victims of the doom and gloom merchants who think 'a dog is only as good as its last retrieve'. That is to say, they do not take all the work into account, and mark within such narrow margins that the most minor slip will result in a dog's dismissal from a Trial.

Recently I was witness to some wonderfully positive judging in a Novice Stake, which makes such a change. There was a partridge down, which had fallen in a ditch, with the wind blowing the wrong way: away from handlers and dogs, through the hedge. In order to pick up the bird the dog had to hunt the ditch, and not only that, hunt it in exactly the right place. I was standing next to the host when the dogs were sent. The first one went through the hedge, hunted in the field the far side and, in the end, went out of control, and the handler had to go forward. The second dog was slower and more careful and at one point it appeared to the host that she had got the bird. 'If she had, she would have been back with it by now' was my comment. Sure enough, the next time she looked through the hedge, she had not got it. The judges had the sense to call her up reasonably quickly. She had had her chance and had not taken advantage of it. The third dog was of extremely high class but had suffered in at least one Novice Stake under the sort of judge who tells the handler where a bird is and then, when it is found somewhere completely different, puts all the dogs concerned out of the Trial. This handler's dog went to the ditch, disappeared briefly through the hedge and was called back. He then hunted the ditch; the first dog to do so. At his second attempt, which followed quickly, he came into the ditch in exactly the right place and picked up the bird. I could have cheered.

Chapter 8

Runners

The difficulty of recovering runners varies enormously, so much so that few present exactly the same problem. No runner is easy to get on a really bad scenting day, but without taking into account atmospheric conditions there are many factors which may have to be taken into consideration when deciding on the real merit of a performance on a runner. At Trials success is the main thing, and a spectacular runner recovered, even though in reality a very easy one, is almost bound to count above failures, however glorious. In fact luck is probably more in evidence where runners are concerned than in any other department at Field Trials. The simplest runner to find is one which falls with a thud, leaving feathers and blood on the spot where it fell. It should run over ground devoid of other scents; it should run straight and keep moving till run into view by the dog. If it is accommodating enough to do all these things on a good scenting day, any puppy should be able to retrieve it. A bird which behaves in this manner may be picked up by a good dog before it has gone one hundred yards, whereas a moderate animal may hunt it slowly for half a mile before he gets it. The slow pottering dog is often given greater credit for his performance than he deserves, and the brilliant dog less. The latter has saved time and disturbed little ground, but has made his job look easy. The former has retrieved what is often asserted to be a wonderful runner.

I can clearly remember two examples of this: once when I was judging; the other when I was running. The first was of a not particularly fast dog taking a runner a very long way. I couldn't help thinking that a more efficient animal would have caught the bird before it got so far, but would it have looked so good? My fellow judges and I agreed that, on the day, we had to give the Trial to the not-so-spectacular dog, which had in fact performed very well indeed throughout.

The second occasion was rather similar. Two bitches were doing very well and likely to finish first and second. The first was sent over a river to a bramble bush in which a runner had been seen taking refuge. The bird ran out of the bush and disappeared round a hill. The bitch eventually followed and came back with it.

When the other bitch was sent, she acknowledged the scent of the first runner (her bramble bush was further away), then continued, when instructed, to the correct bush. The runner and an unshot bird came out on the opposite side to where she was, with the wind blowing away. She ignored the unshot bird, whipped round the bush, and chased and caught her runner with very little delay.

The judges preferred the former performance. This was unfortunate for me for if my bitch, Manymills Milady, had won that Trial, she would have been made up after only her third Open Stake, having already won her first. I was not in the least surprised at the conclusion they reached, and could not blame them at all, having myself made a similar decision on the above-mentioned occasion.

In the *Kennel Club Guide to Judges*, the wording is: 'The task of the judges is to find the dog which, on the day, pleases them most by the quality of its work from the shooting point of view. They should take natural game finding to be of the first importance in Field Trials.' It also states, 'Dogs showing game finding ability and initiative should be placed above those which have to be handled onto their game. Usually, the best dog seems to require the least handling. He appears to have an instinctive knowledge of direction and makes difficult finds look simple and easy.'

It's all there, in the K.C.F.T. regulations which still advise positive rather than negative judging.

A bird more often lost than not is one which settles rather than falls; in fact can almost be said to be running before it touches the ground. Such a bird on a bad scenting day in a field full of other game, if it frequently doubles back on its own tracks, and gets a long start, often beats the first dog sent out for it, and more often still the second. If a third dog can find a bird of this description by following the line, he is a good one.

Sometimes it is an advantage not to be sent first on a runner. One eyewipe by Milady in the two day Open Stake which she eventually won to make her a F.T.Ch. three years after her first win, was achieved when third dog down on a runner. Some instinct, or movement in the beet, suggested to me that it had run back towards the guns. Milady was sent to the fall, and then I watched her follow the scent of the bird back towards the line, where she picked it up about half way between the fall and the guns, handlers etc. Had she been first dog down, I would, like the other handlers, have tried to get her further out rather than nearer to the line. Motto: when in doubt, trust the dog. However, it doesn't *always* work!

Whether or not he was born with a more acute sense of smell than the other two has not been proved. That he owns a scent which the others do not, and is able to discriminate between the right line and many wrong ones has been proved. This ability to discriminate and to follow a runner through a wood, alive with unwounded pheasants, is seldom if ever shown by a young inexperienced dog. The probability is that experience, in some cases coupled with an inherited instinct, will alone make the super runner getter.

I have stated in my book *Retriever Training* that an exceptionally experienced dog on runners, following the line of a pheasant through a wood yet to be driven, does very little, if any, harm, but virtually no gamekeeper will agree. It is certainly true that once the beaters have been though the same wood, maybe half an hour later, the chance of finding the runner is very small, unless one has sufficient dogs to do a carpet-sweep. Much depends upon the size of the area to be covered, and the number of dogs available. Keeping only a small number of dogs and not being a good enough trainer and handler to manage a team, I never have more than three out together, and recognise that under those circumstances I do a less efficient job than people who have teams, and the ability to control them.

The young dog naturally follows the freshest scent, and only practice will teach him that it may be the wrong one. Lack of nose is often given as the reason for a dog's failure to own a stale or faint scent when lack of experience may be the cause. This is proved by the fact that many dogs improve greatly in game finding ability with age, the improvement continuing till quite late in life. This can hardly be due to the senses becoming more acute, but must be the result of experience. Bloodhounds are renowned for their ability to follow a stale scent and for their powers of discrimination. The writer has never trained one, but understands that the results achieved by some of these dogs are only brought about after months of training and experience. An interesting Trial took place in Norfolk some years ago between a Bloodhound which had just won a big Trial, and a Labrador which deservedly had a great reputation as a runner getter. The Labrador won easily, but had the advantage of following his master. The scent was two hours old on a cold windy day in winter.

It might be relevant here to mention my own experience with tracking dogs. A bitch I owned (W.T.Ch. Manymills Tanne, known as Quinta) became a Working Trial Champion by winning two Tracking Dog Open Stakes. Almost all the dogs I owned, until moving to Essex in 1975, had qualifications up to W.D.Ex. Labradors are extremely well suited to Working Trials, particularly the nosework aspect.

Various incidents concerning Quinta spring to mind. As a gundog, she was too hot. She managed to win a two day Open Stake at a ground notorious for its thick bramble. However, when she had her nose down on a human scent, she was oblivious to game. I have seen her flush a partridge and a hare off her track on different occasions and not even raise her head.

When a track is three hours old, all sorts of things can happen to it between the laying and the working. Sometimes the judge follows the competitor round, sometimes he stands most of the time at a vantage point where he can see dog and handler. He has a plan of the track and the tracklayer stands with him.

My husband was once standing with the judge and tracklayer and could see, which I could not, that Quinta had tracked right through a herd of deer which had crossed the track. Someone who now has dogs of my breeding competing in Working Trials had a very similar incident on the New Forest with ponies. The ponies did not actually bother to leave the track and it took some courage on the part of the dog to face them.

While I was still engaged in Working Trials, I was frequently asked if my dogs were better than others, on runners, because of their training. All I can say is, that they were pretty good, but so are dogs I have had since and which have had no Working Trial training. I eventually gave up Working Trials when I moved to East Anglia, because it was impossible to find suitable tracking ground in such an intensively farmed area, and because training a Working Trial dog is far more time consuming than training a gundog. Quinta once followed the line of a heavy retrieving ball 300 yards down a slope of the South Downs, much further than it had been intended to roll, thus saving either me or my husband a very long and hard climb!

The problems presented by scent are innumerable, and the fact is that no one knows much about it. We are here looking at it from the point of view of Field Trials and Judging. It is important, therefore to look into a dog's mind and ask ourselves what it is which enables him to follow one particular line to the exclusion of all others. The usual answer to this question is: 'He follows a blood scent.' Unfortunately blood is absent in the case of a runner quite as often as not. There must, therefore, be some other quality in the scent on which the dog is able to recognise as the right one. Is it that a wounded bird gives off a different scent on account of his wound or through fear? Or is it that each bird has its own individual scent? The writer leans towards the latter explanation as being the most likely, and is to some extent supported in his opinion by the actions of a stoat. This animal, as is well known, will follow one rabbit through hundreds of other rabbits and never leave the line of his intended victim. The rabbit may give off a particular scent through fear, but it seems likely that the first part of the hunt at any rate must have been accomplished by following the individual scent of that particular rabbit. If this is so and individual scent is what a dog has to rely on, the importance of his owning the fall can not be over estimated.

The consistent recovery of runners, particularly of winged partridges in turnips if at all thick, is an art of itself. However successful a dog may be on other ground he will fail more often than not when first taken into a turnip field. Many a good dog has greatly disappointed his owner at Trials mainly held in turnips, purely from lack of experience in that crop. Practice and practice alone will teach a dog to keep the bird always in front of him, and never to overrun it. As a general rule there is a better scent in swedes than in white turnips, but if the swedes are covered with mildew dogs may find difficulty in recovering runners in them. Mustard is another crop which even the experienced dog is quite likely to fail in.

There are days and conditions when the line of a runner can only be followed by the best of dogs for short stretches at a time. This is often noticeable on a hot day on dry fallow, in which occasional thistles and patches of weed are found. One of the most difficult runners the writer ever saw found, was recovered under these conditions. Dog after dog had been tried for a partridge which several guns had seen running across a fallow field. None of them could make anything of it, until an old dog well known to Field Trial men found it. This dog seemed to know at once that there was no scent on the bare fallow, and instead of attempting to follow the line, galloped about from weed to weed and thistle to thistle until he found a spot on which the bird had left a scent.

Scent may not only vary from yard to yard, but also from hour to hour; hence the difficulty of deciding on the real merits of certain performances on runners. That training and experience is largely responsible for ability to follow a line is proved by the prowess of Bloodhounds on the scent of human beings many hours old, of otter hounds on the stale drag of an otter, and of Tufters, though the writer has no knowledge of them, in stag hunting.

The foregoing pages have been written with the object of

showing that training and experience may be as responsible for game finding ability as any inborn acuteness of scenting power. The writer does not deny that there have been and may still be Retrievers and Spaniels born with phenomenal scenting powers, but he cannot be certain that he has ever seen one. On the other hand there are undoubtedly dogs born with indifferent noses, but not nearly so many as is generally supposed. It is safe to assert that were it possible to produce two puppies, similar in every respect, and send them to two different breakers for two years, they would create quite different impressions with regard to their noses in the minds of judges at Trials.

Chapter 9

Pace, Style and Drive

Pace, style and drive are three qualities which judges are entitled to look upon as due to natural ability, i.e. inborn. Of these, pace and drive are worse than useless unless under control, and all three can be ruined by bad breaking or fostered and improved by a capable trainer. Though every dog works in a style of his own, the word style here is intended to refer to a desirable quality. It is easy to recognise but difficult to define in a few words. Perhaps it may be best expressed by saying that style is something in the movements of a dog when working, which gives to the onlooker the impression that the dog is determined and likely to succeed in his task. It is a most attractive gift, and a dog possessing it in a marked degree is always a pleasure to watch, either at Trials or in the shooting field. In fact, style can be said to have been the deciding factor in winning Trials more often than any other quality. It is also probably true that no quality is more likely to be inherited. So much is this the case in some strains that one is frequently able to make a correct guess at the sire or dam of a dog working at some distance away, merely from watching his style. Style in a gundog is much the same thing as eye in a sheepdog, and it cannot be given to a dog which was not born with it. It can, however, be taken away temporarily if not entirely by bad breaking. If a dog loses confidence he is sure to lose his style. The more confidence he gets the more attractive his style becomes. Some young dogs start with no style at all, and develop quite a pleasing amount of it later in life. In Retrievers and Spaniels style shows itself more in stern action and head carriage than anything else, and is usually more pronounced in small dogs than in large ones. As a breed Golden Retrievers have in the past been deficient in style, whereas Labradors are as a rule more stylish than Flat-coats.

Drive is the term generally used to denote a combination of pluck, determination and keenness, and is shown by a dog when facing dense punishing cover, crossing a rapid river in flood and in other ways. Pluck and determination may fairly be classed as attributes due to natural ability, keenness can be created to a great extent by the breaker. Dog breakers with experience will agree that many Spaniels which during their first season sedulously avoid thick cover will often tear through it with apparent enjoyment in their second. This is largely due to sympathetic treatment which has gradually increased the pupil's keenness during his first season to such an extent that any fear of injury to himself is overcome. On the other hand, bad breaking will only make a timid dog worse, and many competitors at Trials which get penalised for refusing to enter punishing cover are less to blame than their trainers. It is not the intention of the writer to write a treatise on dog breaking even were he competent to do so, but the attempt is here being made to show that natural ability is of little use and may not be even apparent to a judge unless fostered or controlled by the breaker's art.

Pace, or rather the kind of pace which every high-class dog must possess, is almost entirely inborn. The breaker may be able to sharpen up a slow dog in many ways, but he cannot give that quickness of movement which at once attracts the favourable attention of judges and spectators alike.

Obviously a fast dog must be placed above a slow one if both are doing the job of collecting all the game for which they are sent. Some judges will eliminate a slow dog at a very early stage, purely on the grounds of its slowness. I would not quarrel with that.

The pace required is more the quickness of a weasel than the galloping powers of the racehorse. Much has been written in the Press condemning pace and arguments have been advanced to show the superiority of the slow dog. It is true that pace which is neither under the control of the dog itself nor its master is most objectionable and should be very heavily penalised. A dog which shows its pace by going too fast for its nose, and heedless of its master's commands, disturbs much unnecessary ground, and is useless for Trials, or in the shooting field. At one time there were very few well broken fast dogs about, and they won most of the Trials. Handlers found that pace was necessary, if they were to have a chance of winning. They therefore looked for and found dogs with pace, and brought them to compete at Trials half broken. Shooting men came to these Trials, saw game being continually driven out of the fields by wild galloping animals, went home disgusted and soon wrote letters to the Press condemning pace and the judges who awarded prizes to fast dogs. Breaking has greatly improved, so much so that several men, who at one time expressed themselves as unable to understand 'this craze for pace', when eventually acting as judges themselves, became the first to penalise and speak of as useless the slow pottering dog. This state of things has been brought about by better breaking and is not in any way due to greater natural ability.

No judge could do anything other than place a fast dog over a slow one, which is even more relevant to Spaniels than Retrievers. To win a Spaniel Trial these days, dogs often have to be on the edge of running in or committing some other crime, and are only controllable by the very best handlers. That is why, when dogs are eliminated in Open Stakes and even the Championship, no one is half as shocked as they would be if a Retriever did something similar. Handlers just have to go home and try to put the matter right. In fact many of them seem to have gone too far, in that some Spaniels hardly dare bring in a live bird because of severe training following the judging methods of the strong anti-pegging lobby.

A well known former judge (now dead) was running a very nice Spaniel under my husband, who remarked what a lovely shooting dog he was (the dog received a certificate of merit). 'Isn't that

68

what Trials are supposed to be about?' asked the handler. They are indeed but how can you not put a faster and more stylish dog over one that does everything needed but less spectacularly?

Having examined the few qualities which must be at least in part due to natural ability, let us look at the other desirable attributes in a shooting dog which are not necessarily inborn.

Take the ability to mark and go straight to the fall from any reasonable distance. This is a knack which is very apt to be inherited, and is reproduced over and over again in certain strains. A dog, however, born without any idea of marking can be taught to mark so effectively that he may easily get the reputation of being a wonderful natural marker.

Many birds are required, or the equivalent in dummies, to teach a bad marker to become a good one. My life is too busy for this, as I am far from a full-time dog trainer. I therefore prefer to breed for marking ability. Some of my dogs hardly bother to mark dummies as they get older, but they usually mark the real thing very well. It is fortunate that they do, as marking in a featureless sea of sugar beet is something at which I am no good at all.

Quartering, or the ability to systematically hunt the whole of a given area, born in nearly all Setters, and in some Retrievers and Spaniels, can be taught so that no one can tell by watching the dog at work whether his ability to quarter was inborn or not. Again a quick clean pick up, natural to some dogs, can be taught, though it may be a long job. In the same way a naturally slow return may be sharpened up. A perfect delivery, if it comes naturally to a puppy, is not so desirable from a breaker's point of view as it seems. Things may go well for a time, but sooner or later a natural delivery is almost certain to deteriorate and trouble will arise when least expected. This is probably due to the fact that the perfect delivery has come from choice and not from necessity, and the natural deliverer sooner or later sees no reason why he should continue to be one. Whereas the puppy which has given some trouble from

69

the start and has been properly taught to deliver, seldom gives cause for anxiety in this respect later.

I have only once had to teach a dog to 'hold'. Other trainers whom I respect, say it should be done in many more cases. Some of my dogs have had a beautiful natural delivery whereas others have not, but all have tended to be better with game than dummies. In trying to cure one fault it is possible to create another and great care should be taken to avoid this.

It is most desirable that a soft mouth should be natural, but a hard one can be cured. The writer knows of several instances where dogs cured of the hardest of mouths have won under judges who were looking for nothing but natural ability. On the other hand, if a puppy has a tendency towards roughness with his game, a hard mouth is easily developed by a mistake in breaking. It would not be an exaggeration to say that hundreds of dogs have been ruined in this way.

I have grave doubts about hard mouth being curable and hope that, in this rare case in which Alington and I disagree, I am right and he was wrong, purely from the breeding and hereditary point of view.

Much might be written about brain, mostly of a theoretical nature, and no attempt will be made to deal with it here at any length. It is certain that the cleverest dogs, those which make the most interesting companions do not necessarily make the best shooting dogs.

The late Bob Baldwin, during an interview, said that he did not like a dog with too much initiative (otherwise there were two captains of the ship) but personally, I have had enormous pleasure over the years from the cleverness of some of my dogs. To give some examples, Manymills Lucky Charm W.D.Ex. U.D.Ex. C.D.Ex. (Pippin) spent six months of her life, while I was working abroad, living in a flat over my brother's photographic studio. He and his wife did not find it at all surprising that she would put her own bones into the rubbish bin on command, something I had certainly never taught her! They also used to take her out and encourage her to chase hares for exercise. Starting her Field Trial career at the age of five, she won three Field Trials and three Open Working Tests. Her earlier life had also included being exercised with my mother's Bull Terriers, part of whose function was the mercy killing of any of the original victims of myxomatosis they came across. She never had her mouth queried during her Field Trial career!

W.T.Ch. Manymills Tanne (Quinta) lived in the house all her life, as did her dam. When I lived in Sussex we had a swimming pool into which she would plunge. Floating in it was a tyre inner tube, on which, from the age of about five months, she succeeded in draping and balancing herself. Not an easy task for any dog, and how did she think of it?

F.T.Ch. Manymills Milady (Millie) showed great brain power when I put a dummy about 3 ft up on a pile of logs. She winded it, but the toggle on the dummy had become jammed in the logs and she had to go round the back of the pile (the wind was blowing in the direction from which I had sent her) to unhook it. There have been many other such examples. Manymills Heron is now an avid TV watcher if there are sheepdog trials, or anything involving a whistle. He stands right in front of the screen, ears up, and listens intently. Gundog training videos are favourite viewing for him, and he also enjoys wildlife programmes.

Judges get very little chance during a Field Trial to test for brain, and must find it impossible to decide what is due to the brain of the dog and what to that of the breaker. Natural ability hunters may justly claim that coolness (no more expressive word suggests itself), one of the most desirable qualities in a gundog, is inborn. Other things being equal coolness should score over excitability, even though the obviously excitable dog is under perfect control. Not because the cool dog is a better one to breed from, which it is submitted is not the business of the judge, but for the reason that he is perhaps less fidgety at heel, or sits stiller during a drive and thus puts up a better performance. Unfortunately, however, the dog which shows no signs of excitement is often deficient in keenness or drive. Luckily, excitable dogs are more difficult to break than cool headed ones, which may account for the fact that a gradual improvement in temperament is taking place.

If anyone has a strain of Spaniels or Retrievers of cool

temperament but full of keenness, combined with good memory and adaptability, they will do well not to lose it.

If only it were that easy. That is precisely what I try to breed for, with varying success. Although my dogs are closely line bred, none turns out identical. The coolest, calmest and easiest to handle was probably Millie, who actually lay down during the duck drive at Ampton in her first Open Stake there, which she won. At least one of the judges was considerably impressed by her calmness, and remarked on it to me. She was virtually perfect in this respect, though even she would once in a while take off after an imaginary runner. No human being is perfect, so why should a dog be expected to be?

Chapter 10

Handling:
Water and other Tests

T he dog which gives us all the greatest pleasure to own, break or handle, is the one which is anxious to please his master, and is not out merely for its own amusement. A dog endowed with a nature of this kind is easier to break and kinder to handle than the purely selfish animal. In fact, from a breeder's point of view, it is one of the most important traits in a dog's character to be considered. Judges, however, would be unable to recognise it with any certainty during a Field Trial.

The writer has more than once listened to arguments between experts as to whether a judge should judge the dog alone, or the performance put up by the dog and handler combined. The dog would be useless without his handler, and it is here submitted that the work of the two combined should be taken into consideration by a judge. Take, for instance, the case of two dogs which do equally meritorious work, but the handler of one is comparatively quiet, whereas the handler of the other makes the welkin ring with his stentorian commands and siren-like whistles. A judge can only come to the conclusion, either that the latter's dog is deaf, or that he has not proved that he can be handled in any other way and must, even if he is attempting to judge the dog only, give preference to the one which has shown that he can be handled quietly. It seems to be as impossible to separate the handler from his dog as it is the horse from his jockey when judging.

Quiet handling is from every point of view much to be

encouraged and may not always receive due recognition from judges. At the same time, it may be well to point out that Trials are not the same as an ordinary day's shooting. It is at times almost impossible to attract one's dog's attention without undue noise at Trials. The line consists of three judges and possibly their sisters carrying their mackintoshes, their stewards, six guns and often their loaders, beaters, number board bearers, officials, press reporters with photographic apparatus, possibly a few dogs on leads and some spectators, besides the six dogs being tried and the handlers. A dog unaccustomed to such a crowd has great difficulty in picking out his handler from among them. If two or three dogs happen to be out working at the same time with the same number of whistles going, it is only fair to make some allowance for the handler who would be considered excessively noisy under different conditions.

The habit some of us have developed, of holding out both arms as the dog returns with a retrieve towards a crowded line, has been heavily criticised in some circles, but as judges nowadays hardly ever allow the handler to step forward well clear of the line, there are few other options when running an inexperienced dog.

Under no circumstances is it fair to prevent a handler from standing out clear from the line or the spectators when handling his dog. Furthermore, an inexperienced handler should always be told that he may do so. During a water test the banks are often lined with spectators. If a difficult test has to be attempted, and it is necessary to guide the dog by signal to a given spot, it is only fair to clear the banks on either side of the handler. Even if this is done it is by no means easy for a dog to pick his handler out when looking back from the water.

The average shooting man, who knows little of the difficulties of managing Field Trials, would probably consider that a good performance in water should be favourably taken into consideration by judges. As a matter of fact, so long as a dog can be induced to swim by any means, water tests seldom affect the awards. It is the exception rather than the rule to find a satisfactory natural water test provided at a Trial, either because there is no suitable water, or because game near it is scarce, the consequence is that artificial tests are resorted to in order to satisfy the judges that dogs will swim. Dead birds are thrown into any available piece of water in full view of the dogs; if any dog refuses to enter the water his handler is often allowed to have a shot fired as an inducement; he may throw in any missiles he can find, and so long as he eventually gets his dog to swim he is seldom penalised for a poor performance. It is here submitted that our open Trials at any rate should have got past this stage, that dogs should enter water freely at the command of their handlers, without any other inducement. When in the water they should demonstrate that they can be guided by signal to any given spot within reasonable distance. The above submission will no doubt be met by the objection that many handlers have no water in which to train their dogs. No allowance is made for the handler who has no woodcock on his ground, if his dog refuses to retrieve one, why then should the absence of water be taken as a good excuse for a bad performance? In order to be strictly fair during an artificial water test all dogs should be kept out of sight of the ones being tried. Many a dog will enter water if given a lead, which he would not have done otherwise.

Water tests are no longer conducted in this way in Retriever Trials. Birds are never thrown in, and every Retriever Championship and many other Stakes, both Open and Novice, contain natural drives into or across water. A Retriever is expected to do more than just enter water and swim. Sometimes dogs are expected to swim up to two hundred yards, often for a bird they have not marked. Not only that, they have to be capable of being handled at these long distances for the correct bird.

Spaniels occasionally have water tests, either natural or artificial. The ability to retrieve from water is a Kennel Club requirement before a dog can be made up to F.T.Ch., as it is also of course for Retrievers, along with a certificate that the latter breeds have sat quietly at a drive. Spaniels are never required to swim as far in their water tests as Retrievers. In fact their test can consist merely of a dead bird being thrown into a pond. Even the best Spaniels tend not to be as easy to handle on water, for direction, as Retrievers.

The H.P.R. breeds, which are outside the scope of this book, always have a water test which is often artificial.

If judges would give favourable consideration to the writer's contention that water tests should be made more severe our Retrievers would soon become more proficient at retrieving game which we cannot gather without them. There is nothing more annoying than seeing, say, a dead duck lying one hundred yards on the other side of a river, and being obliged to leave it there, yet very few judges of the present day, even when they get the chance, will ask a handler to demonstrate that his dog can be got out a hundred yards, even on dry land, and guided when there. Each year adds to the difficulties of judges in coming to their decisions owing to the rise in the general standard of efficiency among competitors. It seems clear therefore that if the same number of dogs are to be judged in the same limited time as at present, tests will have to be made more severe. There have been many good natural water tests provided; among them may be recalled those at Lilford, Dupplin and Didlington; but as might be expected the water tests provided at Adare during the first Irish Retriever Trials affected the awards more than any the writer can remember. In the Open Stake the dog which crossed a flooded river, an osier bed, two wire fences and retrieved a pheasant which had fallen out of sight over a hill, deservedly won.

In the Non-Winners Stake three dogs were level for third place; time was short; a snipe had fallen ten yards over the same flooded river. None of the three dogs, judging from their previous performances, seemed likely to get the snipe. The judges therefore decided to place the dog third which got nearest to it. One of the three got half way across the river and won by a yard.

Although the writer is an advocate of severer tests, there

is one which it is inadvisable if not unfair to set. A handler should never be asked to send his dog a long way *dead into the wind* for game which it has not marked. It is easier to get a dog out two hundred yards downwind than fifty against it, and though a dog can be taught to go into the wind, it is all against a very desirable instinct which he possesses. In spite of what has been said and written to the contrary, every dog naturally gives himself the wind; that is to say, goes downwind of the spot where he hopes to find something by means of his nose. When hunting for something *he has not seen* he dislikes going far into the wind for fear of leaving the scent behind him. In the writer's opinion it is very unwise to force him to do so beyond certain limits. It cannot be denied that circumstances may arise when it is most useful to be able to send one's dog a long way into the wind for something which he has not seen and cannot wind till he gets near it, but a dog taught to do it, may be to some extent spoiled in the process. If anyone owns what he considers to be a handy dog, it is always safe to bet that he cannot send his dog a hundred yards into a stiff breeze by signal or word of command alone.

In modern Field Trials and Working Tests, Retrievers are expected to handle out a long distance into the wind. Most judges never give a thought to the difficulty this presents, or the damage it causes to the instinct of the dog to 'sink the wind', that is, to go downwind of a mark, and sometimes a very long way downwind, according to the amount and strength of the wind. Some judges would even penalise this on the grounds of bad and inaccurate marking. I hope Mrs Gabrielle Benson will not mind me quoting some words she wrote on this topic, 'I disagree that my dog has not marked well because it sinks the wind on the way out to the fall. I am concerned that we are stifling nose and instinct in favour of creating robotic guided missiles.'

One of the most frequent causes of complaint by handlers, and sometimes a justifiable one, is that they have been wrongly directed as to the spot where game fell. What often happens is that one of the guns shoots a bird unseen by the judge, who may be watching the work of a dog elsewhere. The judge is informed that a bird is down; the exact spot where it fell is pointed out to him by the gun, who has probably forgotten where it did fall, and may be anything from ten to fifty yards out in his reckoning. The spot indicated by the shooter is pointed out to the handler, who works his dog accordingly and fails to find the bird. By this time many different opinions as to where the bird did actually fall will have been given, and eventually a second or third dog may find it, stone dead, thirty or forty yards downwind of where it was originally said to be lying. Circumstances such as these place judges in a difficult position from which they must extricate themselves in their own way. The writer himself when judging makes it a rule never to send for a bird which is said to have fallen a long way out, and which has been seen by no one but the shooter, who may be optimistic. When reasonably certain that a bird is down, which he has not seen fall, he gives the handler the information given by the gun, at the same time informing him that he cannot guarantee its accuracy.

This sort of situation still arises very frequently at Trials and causes more heart-burning than almost anything else. Some judges, looking for any excuse to put a dog out, to make their own task easier, will eliminate any dog which fails to find a bird no matter how inaccurate the original mark, and how far away the bird is eventually picked. Once, when judging a driven Trial on partridges, we judges were reliant on some of the worst markers I have ever come across and were continually having to forgive dogs for failing to find birds which were nowhere near where we had been told. However, I was not impressed with the sportsmanship of one competitor who immediately said, when a bird was found well outside the area that had been indicated to him, 'That is nowhere near where I was told', before my fellow judge and I had time to say that we had no thoughts of putting him out. Competitors should wait to find out the judges' intentions before lodging a complaint.

The result of the bad marking was that the Trial took a lot longer to judge than it should have done. Societies which are forced by their geography to have virtually all their Trials on drives are usually much more efficient at getting a good marker for almost every gun, which is what is required. It is neither the gun's job to mark, nor the judges'. They both have other things to do although clearly it can, to a point, be a combined operation.

Those who are about to judge for the first time will be well advised to make reasonably certain that there is game to find before sending a dog to find it. Anxiety to discover something on which judges can try a competitor often has a stimulating effect on the imagination of spectators. Birds are reported to have fallen, and hares and rabbits to have died, which are in reality in the best of health. Novice judges should also make certain that game which is known to have fallen has not been picked up either by a beater or by a dog working under another judge. This is not an uncommon occurrence at Trials, and not only wastes time but is unfair to the dog and handler asked to look for what is not there. If in doubt as to whether a bird is down or not it is better to get the keeper to send someone to look for it than to send a competitor to do so. A failure on the part of the competitor only creates a doubt in the judges' mind and a feeling of injustice in the mind of the handler.

Ground is occasionally given for Trials by generous owners so well stocked with game that it is at times surplus to the requirements of judges. In such circumstances men with dogs not competitors are usually, and should always, be left behind to pick up after the judges have made use of what they require.

As a rule however every head of game shot is wanted for judging purposes. There are thousands of head of game shot during the season by shooting parties to every head killed at Trials, and the writer, who has had some experience of both, is convinced that the proportion of dead and wounded game lost at Trials is far less than during ordinary shooting days. He would even go further than that and assert that an attempt is made to recover a larger proportion of crippled game at Trials than is the case during shooting days throughout the country.

If a handler has not seen the game he is to be sent for shot, it is only fair and expedient that he should have the fall pointed out to him as nearly as possible. Fair because the handler who is to be given the second chance, if the first fails, may have been in a position to mark the fall exactly. Expedient from the judge's point of view, because the handler, knowing where he should work his dog, has no excuse for disturbing half the field. The writer cannot help being a little suspicious of the handler who never by any chance knows where game falls, even if shot right in front of his nose. This apparent blindness may or may not be a form of hedging against a failure to find the game, or to get the dog near to the desired spot. There are some handlers who never whistle, either in order to gain credit for quiet handling, or because their charges would take no notice if they did.

This reminds me of a very clever handler of the past, the late Dick Male. If his dog took no notice at the first whistle, he kept silent. On one occasion his dog overshot the fall of a runner, and met the bird on the way back when the latter had left the beet and appeared to be in pursuit of the dog. Not many of us experience luck like that in Trials! But could it all be put down to luck, or the genius of a quite exceptional trainer and handler?

If a dog is careering about far from the spot where the game is known to be, a judge can only come to the conclusion that the latter reason is the correct one.

There is no doubt that prizes should not be awarded to any dog at a Trial which has not been seen by the judges at a drive. Deportment during a drive is of great importance nowadays, and it may provide for some dogs the greatest test of steadiness. There are dogs which never give themselves away while game is being walked up, but which whine and even bark with excitement during a drive. A runner falling in full view of a dog at a drive has often proved its undoing, although it may have remained steady while walking cover in line. Unfortunately, drives take up a lot of valuable time, and the game finding tests provided after them are often unsatisfactory; the consequence is that where game can be shot in cover by walking in line, then drives often have to be dispensed with when time is short. There are Trials, however, when driving is the only method by which game can be killed. In such cases the novice judge will be well advised not to place implicit trust in the arithmetical powers of the shooters. He will find that they seldom arrive at a figure which is less than the total of the slain. Sometimes indeed an optimistic shooter has been known to believe that he has killed several more birds than he actually has. His mistake may lead not only to a waste of time, but also to hardship on the competitor which may have failure marked against him unfairly. A judge's attention is often taken up by the dogs under him, so that he is not always in a position to see for himself what is killed; his steward, however, is disengaged, and may be induced to mark down roughly on a piece of paper the number and locality of the birds shot.

Not all Trials today incorporate drives, not even all Open Stakes, but it is impossible to make up a F.T.Ch. without a certificate that it has sat quietly at a drive. There are, however, drives and drives. Sometimes dozens or even hundreds of birds come over in a drive lasting half an hour and many are shot. On other occasions a drive might last a few minutes with only one or two birds killed.

Among the many difficult problems which a judge has at times to solve is the case of the wounded bird located by a dog, which gets up again and flies. In such a case the dog may (1) stand still and watch it (2) he may chase it and catch it (3) he may chase it out of sight and lose it, or (4) he may chase it for a shorter distance and give it up as a bad job. The writer, while in no way wishing to influence the opinions of other judges, would deal with the matter in this way.

(1) The dog has found the bird and shown steadiness, so must be duly credited.
(2) So long as the handler does not attempt to stop him the dog must get a credit mark; if the handler whistles, no mark.

81

(3) If the handler tries to stop the dog, a debit mark; if he does not, no mark.

(4) Must gain a credit mark; the dog may either return to whistle, or because he has sense enough to see that he cannot catch the bird.

Personally, I would credit (2) above (1) on the grounds that a wounded bird should be put into the bag, but the opinion of a man I respect highly, Bob Walker, is that once a dog is allowed to chase a flying bird, the writing is on the wall for future discipline. Most judges would eliminate (3) and (4).

The word 'mark' in the above lines is used merely for explanatory purposes, and must not be taken to mean that the writer actually uses or believes in the use of marks for judging purposes.

It is entirely in the hands of the judges whether shooting takes place while a dog is out working or not. Some judges say no, others order indiscriminate shooting. Again, others ask the guns to shoot birds which will not fall near a dog working. There are pros and cons for all these points of view. If no shooting takes place when any dog is out working, all competitors are treated alike. If indiscriminate shooting goes on some dogs are subjected to far more severe tests than others. The same applies to a lesser extent when guns try to drop birds away from the working dog. In Open Stakes the writer himself would have no hesitation in advocating indiscriminate shooting if the guns would carry out their instructions. The trouble is that some will shoot and others, perhaps interested in watching the work of the dogs, will not. The result is that a legitimate cause of complaint by handlers arises. Handler A considers it unfair that Gun 1 should drop a bird close to his dog when working, whereas Gun 2 did not even fire at a bird which might have fallen close to Handler B's dog. The question is a difficult one, but on the whole the writer is of opinion that in Open Stakes game should be shot as in an ordinary day's shooting. Dogs which are under sufficient control to withstand the severest tests of steadiness occasioned thereby should be duly credited, and the others penalised according to the temptation. It is admitted that this mode of procedure would introduce another large element of luck into Field Trials, but, as has been stated before, no one seriously objects if they can attribute their dog's failure to bad luck. There is so much luck about all these competitions that the addition of a little more gives a greater number of competitors a chance of getting a share. If there was no luck at all about Trials there would be comparatively few dogs' names in the prize-lists, and Trials would soon die out for want of competitors. If the above method became universal in Open Stakes considerable assistance would be given to the judges in what becomes annually a more difficult task.

This is as intractable a matter now as ever it was. Nowadays, the guns sometimes include people who also run in Trials, and the way they shoot, or refrain from shooting birds while dogs are out working, can have a great deal of influence on the outcome of the Stake.

As far as guns who do not compete in Trials are concerned, it is up to sensible judges to decide what to do. Guns should always be asked not to shoot directly over a dog while it is out working. If they ignore this advice, judges should decide what is proper and reasonable for a dog to have done under the circumstances. In a recent Championship, which had the advantage of sensible and practical judges, F.T.Ch. Quail of Gunstock was in full gallop towards his bird when another was dropped right in front of him. Naturally he picked it up, and naturally, under those judges, he was forgiven.

A few years ago two or three dogs almost invariably stood out from the others, and up to twenty dogs could be judged in the day. It is not so at the present time, when after a long day, judges are often at their wits' end to make their awards in a twelve dog Stake.

Among their other duties judges are called upon to award handlers' certificates if sufficient merit is shown to deserve them. If these certificates could be given to the breaker instead of the handler it would be more appropriate. Handling is often said to play a large part in the winning of a Trial, when in reality breaking should have had the credit. The finest handler in the world is helpless unless his dog is under control and will answer his signals. If a dog's education is properly finished handling him is easy; but the breaker deserves the credit. It is true that handlers are frequently called upon to make important decisions at a moment's notice, but in the majority of such cases, be they experts or novices, they are just as likely to be wrong as right.

A curious incident occurred a few years ago when the writer got the better of the greatest expert he has ever known. A private Trial was in progress, a partridge, apparently stone dead, fell in some turnips and the writer's dog, which had not seen the bird, was sent for it. The dog at once struck a line and raced down a drill; one of those momentous decisions had to be made; was the bird after all a runner? The dog, however, was left alone and returned from the far end of the field with – a live rabbit. The expert, who was acting as judge, was some distance away, so the writer shouted: 'Do you knock him out?' As no one had shot at a rabbit all morning, and it was therefore very unlikely to be wounded, the answer came back: 'Yes.' When, however, the rabbit was brought up for inspection it was found that a snare was wound round its foreleg on which there was blood. The previous decision was at once reversed, and the handler's mistake luckily escaped the penalty.

If only today's judges were willing to admit to mistakes and put them right on the spot, it would make such a difference to the atmosphere and sportsmanship of Trials. However, the modern attitude seems to be 'I am infallible'. Not true – not of anyone.

The writer has committed many errors of judgment when handling his dogs at Trials, but after thinking them all over it seems probable that there have been about as many instances where he has failed to call his dog off when he should have done so, as there have been when he has whistled when the dog should have been left alone.

One of the most nerve racking times for a handler who

is hunting his dog for a bird which may or may not be a runner occurs when a hare or rabbit, possibly slightly wounded, is seen to pass near the fall of the bird. If the dog, finding no dead bird, starts off on a line, what can a handler do? The only answer to this and to many of the other problems which will arise, is trust to his dog and his luck.

Today's answer, under almost all judges, would be that the dog must confine himself to the original bird for which he was sent, possibly leaving a wounded bird ungathered. This is unfortunate.

Chapter 11

Spaniel Trials

Though the foregoing chapters have dealt primarily with Retriever Trials, much of what has been written applies equally to Spaniels where the retrieving part of their work is concerned.

A few Trials have been held for Spaniels working as retrievers only, in which they have not been asked to act as beaters as well. Useful as these Trials are, the winners of them are not eligible to run in the Spaniel Championship, and the following remarks are not intended to apply to them.

My experience from about 1965 to 1990, after which mixed Trials were no longer run by the Utility Gundog Society, is relevant here. When I was running Labradors in Utility Trials, which was most of the time, I always thought the Retriever judges bent over backwards in order to treat the Spaniels well, and I still think that, after running a Spaniel for a few years myself. Not only that, but most societies included a Spaniel judge. To me that was about as logical as including a Sheepdog Trial judge, if an attempt was to be made to run a sheepdog as a gundog, as once happened in a Utility Trial when a sheepdog was entered as a Crossbred. In those days Crossbred Retrievers (e.g. Golden/Labrador) were permitted by the Kennel Club, but if the sheepdog had got into the awards I think there might have been problems! As all the dogs were being judged on their ability as Retrievers, surely only Retriever judges need have been invited?

Many of them would remark 'Oh, I do love Spaniels', and some of their judgments were affected. Anything a Spaniel does looks faster and more stylish than most Retrievers, because of their smaller size and hunting style. The flapping ears when returning with a retrieve also drew favourable comments! There was a rather boring (to my eyes) Spaniel which won the Herts, Beds and Bucks Utility on three consecutive occasions. The first time, I was judging (when the Spaniel and the Golden Retriever ran off on a non-existent bird) but for the other two occasions I take no responsibility and was running a Labrador myself both times.

As was the case when discussing Retriever Trials, the writer has no intention or wish to attempt to influence the opinions of judges as to what part of a dog's work they should lay the greatest stress on. Different methods of judging, however, will be discussed, and arguments in favour of some of them, on the score of equity, advanced.

Stakes for single Spaniels are the most popular. In these, dogs run against each other as drawn and printed on the card, one against two, and so on until they have all been tried once. The judges then pair them as they think best for further trial.

Some years ago a long discussion took place in the *Field* newspaper, in which the writer took a leading part, though his name did not appear in it, between two schools of thought. On the one side were ranged a considerable body of Field Trial men, which we will call the old school. On the other, to which the writer belonged, was the new school. The old school, which probably still has adherents, expressed the opinion that in single Stakes for Spaniels the handlers should be told by the judges to walk together, and that their dogs should be made to hunt and quarter the same ground.

Nowadays Spaniels hunt separately, but ideally not too far apart, in the body of the Stake, and only hunt the same ground (or right next to each other) during a run-off.

The chief argument used in favour of this method of judging was that it was easier to compare the merits of two dogs in this way, and that superiority in game finding ability was more surely detected. In spite of there being a certain amount of truth in their argument, the new school were equally as strongly of the opinion that handlers should be far enough apart to give each dog a reasonable width of ground to hunt without needing to infringe on the ground of his opponent. The arguments they advanced are as strong today as they were when this discussion was published. In the first place, a single Stake is not a Brace Stake, and there are two handlers, not one. When these two handlers are walking close together, particularly if their signals happen to be somewhat alike, it is most confusing and maybe most unfair to the dogs. A noisy handler must inevitably spoil the work of the dog whose handler is accustomed to working his dog quietly. Again there are many Spaniels which are high-class workers alone, but which will not work in conjunction with another dog, either from jealousy, excitability or want of practice. Are these dogs, which are most useful to the average shooting man, to be to all intents and purposes barred from competing in single Stakes, by what the writer believes to be the wrong system of judging?

Take the case of the man who only owns one dog and has no means of giving it any experience of working with another. The chances are that, if he brings it to a Trial, and is told to work it with another dog, a complete stranger, on the same ground, it will be all at sea. The object of a single Stake should be to demonstrate what a single Spaniel can do, working as a single Spaniel would work, on an ordinary day's shooting.

As has already been pointed out, a Spaniel which had never worked with another dog or dogs would nowadays be considered improperly trained and prepared for Trials and would hardly last five minutes, thus wasting a nomination. It is open to anyone to take his dog beating or to meet with friends for practice.

It is true that some of the ground to be found at Trials may be of such a nature that, if two dogs are kept down on it, they will have to work together. When this is the case it seems only fair that judges should treat with leniency faults which were not in evidence when the dogs were each working their own ground.

Some judges are more impressed by a quick pick up, fast

return and perfect delivery than are others, who lay greater stress on the importance of game finding ability. It may have escaped the notice of the former that a Spaniel must find game once before his master can have any sport at all, and twice before there can be any delivery. When comparing the retrieving of two Spaniels, it is only right to take into consideration the length of time a dog has been working, and the nature of the cover he has been through. Five minutes spent in tearing through dense brambles will take more out of a dog than half an hour of easy going. The fresher a dog is the better and quicker his retrieving is likely to be.

In the same way, when comparing the pace of two competitors while quartering and hunting, the previous work done by both, and the length of time for rest each has been given, should be carefully taken into consideration.

Stakes for Braces and Teams no longer exist.

Though Single Stakes are now being discussed it may be as well to draw attention to the fact that dogs running therein may have their chances in a Brace or Team Stake, run subsequently, seriously affected. It is a well-known axiom that anything which occurs in one Stake shall have no bearing on the awards in another. Thus if a dog happened to be discarded for hard mouth in a Non-Winners' Stake he would start with a clean sheet in the Open. This is only fair and as it should be, but it is here suggested that there may be an exception to this rule, where Brace or Team Stakes are concerned. Let us suppose that Mr A enters a Brace or Team, and also enters each individual member of them in a single Stake, which is run first. Mr B also enters a Brace or Team, but reserves them entirely for these Stakes. In such a case the writer considers that no notice should be taken of the running in the single Stake, and that although Mr A's dogs may have had most of the steam taken out of them when running in it, no allowance should be made for their condition. In fact, Mr B should derive any advantage there may be from having saved his dogs for the Brace or Team Stakes. On the other hand, if both owners enter any of the individual members of their Braces or Teams in the single Stake, it seems only fair that the amount of work done in that Stake should be taken into account by the judges, in the Brace or Team Stake run subsequently. The judges themselves are solely responsible for the length of time a competitor is kept working. It may be that Mr A's Brace get a terrible gruelling in the single Stake, whereas Mr B's may get off lightly. This is not a matter of luck; the judges are responsible for it, and should take it into consideration when the Brace or Team Stake is run.

It is a great pity that there are not more braces and teams entered at Trials. They are most interesting from a spectator's point of view, and require more patience and a higher form of education from the breaker. One reason for the waning popularity of braces and teams may be that they take longer to bring to perfection and cannot be as readily sold as the single Spaniel. Again a brace or team cannot well be broken or handled without the use of the voice, unless the breaker uses a different whistle for each member of his team, a feat which as far as the writer knows has not yet been attempted. Rightly or wrongly the human voice is said to be more disturbing to game than the whistle, and is certainly less likely to escape adverse criticism from most judges. The consequence is that the handler who reserves his dogs for single Stakes only obtains an advantage on the score of quietness over the man who breaks them to run in teams.

Of late years it seems to have become the practice of handlers to allow, and of judges to expect, Spaniels to follow the line of ground game from the flushing point to the spot where it was killed or wounded; in fact to follow the line of an unwounded animal, often for very considerable distances.

This is very interesting, as what might be described as 'present day judges of the old school' still prefer to see a dog take the line of a rabbit from where it was flushed to where it was shot. Obviously, in the case of a running pheasant the dog should take the line. Not being a Spaniel expert I would hesitate to express an opinion, but if I did, it would be that the dog should take the quickest and most effective route from flush to shot.

A failure on the part of a competitor to own and hold such a line is often penalised, and – in the writer's opinion – wrongly penalised by judges. Theoretically the following of a line of an unwounded animal by a Retriever or Spaniel is wrong, though it must be admitted that where Spaniels are concerned, the practice saves trouble in breaking and often time in the recovery of game. The last thing the breaker of a Retriever would do would be to encourage him to follow the line of a hare or rabbit before it had been wounded. His chief object is to teach his dog to discriminate between scents, and not to follow any line he happens to come across. Many Spaniel breakers, however, encourage what the Retriever breaker would consider disastrous. They do so for several reasons. In the first place the following of the line from the flushing point favourably impresses some judges. It often saves time, and it relieves the breaker from the necessity of making his dog handy, i.e. teaching him to work by signal where he wants him to work. Both with Spaniels and Retrievers this is the longest job a dog breaker has to tackle, and there is no wonder that any dodge for eliminating this part of his work is taken advantage of. There are, however, occasions when the handler who resorts to the line hunting method only of gathering his game is at a disadvantage. In the event of his dog putting three or four rabbits out of one bush, which all run in different directions, and only one is shot, the odds are against his dog choosing the right line. Again, if told to hunt for game flushed by his opponent, there may be no line for the dog to follow, and unless the handler is able to put his dog quickly where he wants him, by signal, much time may be wasted. The writer admits that he has followed the prevailing fashion, and allows his Spaniels to follow what may be termed the live line, but when judging he would never penalise a dog for failing to do so, provided he was quickly guided to the desired spot, and owned the wounded line.

It is quite common, even in the present day, to see Spaniels in Trials (particularly Novice Stakes) which have little or no idea of being handled. It is an enormous disadvantage to them unless they are extremely lucky.

It is a common thing at Spaniel Trials to see game, mostly rabbits, put up by spectators after the dogs have worked the ground and behind the judges. Though it is possible that these rabbits should have been found by the competitors, and that they deserve a penalty for failing to do so, it is probable that judges will be acting in the best interests of equity by ignoring the game thus flushed. A judge cannot tell exactly where a rabbit which gets up behind him was flushed and therefore cannot be certain whether the dog under him should have found it or not. His attention is drawn to some game put up in this way, but not to all; the consequence is that one competitor may get penalised and another, equally guilty of missing game, escapes. Again, spectators may be more numerous behind one dog than another, and are thus more likely to show up his omission.

This happens possibly more often at the Spaniel Championship than any other Trial and, as Alington suggests, makes for difficult decisions by judges. The reason it happens so often in the Championship is partly that the line is almost invariably too wide, owing to the custom of fitting in five guns instead of four, to the crowds walking behind and to the photographers and others actually in the line or just behind it. It is extremely difficult for the judges concerned to come to right and fair decisions, and Alington is probably correct in saying that almost all such incidents should be ignored, unless blatant 'missing' takes place on the dog's own beat.

The writer judged at two Trials where beaters were provided, who walked in line behind the dogs in order to show the judges what game had been missed: the object being to obtain equality of treatment for each dog. As some of these beaters were energetic, and others decidedly not, little or no help was provided by the procedure.

What a horrifying idea!

It is generally accepted that a Spaniel should work mute on all occasions, and there is no doubt that a dog which continually gives tongue should be ruled out. Judges must decide for themselves to what extent they will penalise an occasional lapse of this nature. Some very keen dogs will give an occasional yelp in thick cover, in their anxiety to get through it; also when chasing a lightly wounded rabbit. The writer has known several good Spaniels which invariably gave tongue when swimming out to game they could see on the water. It seems a little unreasonable that an otherwise first class dog should be very heavily penalised for a fault which cannot adversely affect the bag. On the other hand, it may be argued that this fault is hereditary, and we do not want a breed of tongue throwing Spaniels.

Judges have become much more severe about the matter of a Spaniel making any sort of noise, under any circumstances. In fact many of them seem even more severe than the Retriever judges, who will allow the odd squeak or whine, and quite rightly so in my opinion. It is back to the same old story of looking for the good points in dogs instead of merely the bad ones.

My decision to stop running Layerbrook Guinea in Field Trials was the result of her having been put out for letting out one yip when she was out of sight in cover. I do not know what caused her to do it, but decided it was pointless to travel many miles to an Open Stake to run the risk of that happening again. In fact she settled down and became a calm, quiet, picking up dog for many years. Unlike my Labradors she would get up and walk about a bit so that she could peer round, for example, a partridge butt, but for almost all the rest of her life she was completely steady and quiet, and a joy to own and handle.

While on the subject of noise, it is heartening that in the 1960s a Golden Retriever bitch won a Trial (one of the judges was June Atkinson) by barking at a runner which she had chased up a tree. Without the barking, the bird would never have been in the bag.

Even then, I thought it a brilliantly sensible decision, but how many of today's judges would have come to the same conclusion?

It is only lately that water tests for Spaniels have become at all general, and the writer well remembers much dissatisfaction being shown by some handlers when a water test was insisted on during a Champion Stake not many years ago. A Spaniel is just as likely to be required to enter water as a Retriever, and if the buyer of one of our Field Trial winners were to find that his new purchase would not enter water he would be unlikely to buy another, and the standard of work required to win one of our Trials would soon get the reputation of being a low one.

As in the case of Retrievers, some judges are apt to give the first dog down after a running bird or legged rabbit too much time to recover it. After repeatedly failing to own or hold the line, the handler is often allowed to cast his dog forward, at the same time walking over the line and fouling it for the next dog. If after failing to own the line, or after following it for a short distance and returning to his handler, the dog is called up and another tried, judges would find it much less difficult to arrive at their decisions than they do when the chance of the second dog has been ruined.

The writer has often been asked whether a Spaniel should actually drop to shot when flushing game, or whether a standing position is equally satisfactory. This, of course, must depend on the individual opinions of judges. The writer's own opinion is that so long as the dog is motionless directly the game is flushed or driven out of cover, it does not matter whether he sits or stands. A dog, which goes several yards after game which has been so flushed or driven out, is not so well finished, or so pleasant to shoot over, as one which drops or stops instantaneously.

The extent to which a Spaniel should be penalised for catching an unwounded rabbit is another problem which judges are often called upon to decide. This again is largely a matter of individual opinion and the circumstances in

94

each particular case. A judge will consider whether the dog drops the game uninjured, immediately on command. Whether he makes a continual practice of catching game; and the nature of the cover in which the game was caught. Whether the rabbit was particularly loth to be dislodged. Whether the dog's chief aim seems to be to catch game rather than drive it into the open. There seem to be occasions when a dog should incur no penalty for what in different circumstances may become a flagrant offence. It should be remembered however, that a dog which catches rabbits in punishing cover, such as dense brambles, is likely to face such thickets with more drive and determination that others which never commit the offence.

All judges will probably agree that a Spaniel should quarter the ground he is hunting without undue vocal or pedestrian assistance from his handler. Though it is possible for quartering to become too stereotyped and artificial, there are many otherwise good Spaniels running in Trials today which seem to have little idea of making their ground good without the assistance of their handlers. The best dog to kill game over is one which does all the beating himself and leaves his handler nothing to do but walk straight ahead and pay all his attention to the shooting.

Judges should remember, however, when comparing the quartering abilities of different competitors that the direction of the wind during each dog's trial is an all-important factor. Most dogs if they quarter at all will do so in the most convincing manner when working dead against the wind. When working downwind they must of necessity keep casting out and working the ground back to their handlers. If working on a side wind a dog which quarters beautifully against the wind can hardly be said to be quartering at all, though hunting perfectly. If in doubt about two dogs it is therefore always as well to put them down together, so that they can be seen under the same conditions of wind. One often hears it said that so and so could not get his dog out when asked to retrieve something which the dog had not seen shot. Here again the wind makes all the difference, and a failure to go out against the wind is far more excusable than it would have been on a side or downwind.

The question has arisen whether Spaniels should be asked to submit to the ordeal of sitting at a drive during Trials in which the competitors are expected to beat as well as retrieve. It must be admitted that a dog which will sit quietly during a drive is a more useful animal, all else being equal, for general purposes, than one which whines or even barks. It may be pointed out, however, that if driving tests were to become general at Trials, many otherwise first class dogs would not pass them nor would their owners enter them to compete. The writer himself is in favour of raising the standard of efficiency required at Trials, but is doubtful whether we have yet arrived at a stage when a driving test should be made part of an ordinary Spaniel Trial. It may be that in the near future, as the difficulty of separating competitors increases, driving tests will be most useful, and there is no doubt that dogs which can pass them satisfactorily are the ones required by a large number of shooting men.

I think it is true to say that Spaniels are never asked to sit at a drive in Trials today though I do remember competing in one which started with a duck drive, but the dogs were all on leads out of the way. They were then asked to collect the duck in the form of unseen retrieves. This was unusual, but not to my mind unfair, especially as my own bitch excelled at that sort of task!

Field Trials today are more serious affairs than they were when the writer first competed at them, and judges' decisions may have more far reaching effects. It behoves them therefore to spare themselves no trouble in order to endeavour to see every incident which occurs during the Trial of the dogs under them. Things happen at the most unlikely moments which if seen by the judge may make all the difference to the awards, and which if unseen may give a competitor an unfair advantage. Judges on the whole are most painstaking, but it is a fact that a Trial is seldom concluded without some handler audibly thanking his stars that the judge failed to see his dog doing something for which he might have been penalised, or expressing a fear that the judge was not in a position to see the exceptional brilliance of some of his dog's work.

Perhaps I could mention here the campaign by some of us to have four judges for the Spaniel Championship? It is highly relevant to the points that Alington is making.

As has been said before, the writer believes firmly that all judges try to give fair decisions, though very naturally his opinion does not always coincide with those of the judges. Competitors at Trials will do well to cultivate the same belief and not to take it too much to heart when they are not awarded all they think they deserve. The writer himself has run with varying results at many Trials, and has come to the conclusion that the only thing that really matters is the behaviour of his dog. If an owner is satisfied with his dog's performance he should go home pleased. If the performance also pleases the judges he may go home more pleased. If his dog runs badly or not up to its home form let him endeavour to show him to better advantage next time.

This is excellent advice, and not only for Spaniel handlers.

Chapter 12

What Field Trials
Have Done

I t is more freely admitted today than it was a few years
ago among the general body of shooting men that Field
Trials have done something to improve our gundogs.
This is probably due to the fact that the average work at
Trials is better, and that more shooting men have attended
Trials and seen the improvement. What have Field Trials
actually done? The writer's memory can take him no farther
back than the year 1881, when at the age of nine he was
given his first game licence. It was on the 1st of September
that, accompanied by two male relations, the keeper, a
youth to carry game, and a Retriever, he set out to shoot at
his first partridge. At the start no one took much notice of or
interest in the semi-curly Retriever which rejoiced in the
name of 'Crasher'. The keeper, however, showed much
concern at the temporary loss of his slip which consisted
of a leather strap to which was attached a length of rope.
When found the strap was fastened round his ample
and velveteen covered waist, and 'Crasher' attached by a
wooden contrivance to the rope. The writer later discovered
that this contrivance was most expeditious for the release of
'Crasher,' but useless for getting him back. Not many yards
of the first field had been walked when a single bird got up.
After an excited yell of 'Mark, Master Charles' from the
keeper, the writer hastily discharged his gun into the air,
and the bird fell. Everyone was petrified with astonishment
at the keeper, who proceeded somewhat unwillingly, but
dragged by 'Crasher' to the fall.

Even today, some of us have come across the equivalent of 'Crasher' and his owner, but fortunately they are becoming rarities.

The field was one of standing clover, and neither 'Crasher', still fixed to the rope, nor his master was able to find the bird. The writer, in an agony of apprehension lest his first and probably only bird, should be lost, begged for the release of 'Crasher' who had ceased to take any interest in the proceedings. 'Crasher' at large, became a different animal. He seemed to be quite aware that hares lived in that field as well as partridges. He chased the first he found over a railway and escaped death from an express train by a miracle. On his return he saw to it that no hare was left undisturbed in that field, and incidentally cleared it of partridges. The youth found the lost bird, and the party adjourned to another field. The writer's experience of other shooting parties away from home was not at that time extensive, but there is reason to believe that the above was not an uncommon experience in those days. The Retriever was then looked upon as a necessary evil, and was seldom off the lead until the guns had left the field when some very useful work in picking up was done.

During the last forty-eight years changes in the status of our gundogs have been gradually taking place. When Field Trials for Retrievers were started there were not many really steady dogs to be seen. One of them, even if it never went out of a walk, was almost sure of a place in the award list. Each year, however, saw an improvement which was gradual until the arrival of Mr A. E. Butter (as he was then) on the scene. He was the pioneer of a big jump forward, and was able to demonstrate with 'Peter of Faskally', and many others, what a dog's education should be, and the advantages of so educating him. He has had many followers since, but as far as the writer has seen, no equal. The methods of shooting have changed since 1881, but whether we look at a day's partridge driving or a rough day's walking after a mixed bag, the change from 'Crasher' and his like is very apparent. Gone is the slip, and as a general rule the necessity for it. Instead of a few furtive looking half-wild animals tied to their masters, many of the guns now own dogs which they take the greatest pride and pleasure in, and which at all events will not ruin the day's shooting. Instead of being necessary evils, dogs have become for many a very pleasurable part of the day's proceedings. A man who owns a really good dog, even if shooting badly, can always feel that he has played his part in adding to the bag, and can look back with pleasure on the good work done by his dog. Much of this change for the better in the social position of our gundogs and in the pleasure which they give is due to the Field Trial movement. To it also can be attributed the great increase in numbers of both men and women who understand dogs, and are capable of breaking them. Largely owing to the higher form of education dogs have had for Field Trial competitions, each succeeding generation has become more easily trained. It is said to be a scientific fact that training can have no effect on the progeny of the trained. If scientists had had the same experience of breaking generation after generation of gundogs as the writer, or of sheepdogs as many shepherds have had, their views would probably be modified. No one is likely to deny that Field Trials have been the means of improving the education of gundogs, particularly Spaniels and Retrievers, beyond recognition, but have they done anything to improve nose or game finding ability? This is a difficult question to answer, and there are many more capable of answering it than the writer. There were in pre-trial days a few dogs with great reputations as game finders. There are probably more in 1929. The best nosed dogs of today have had no superiors in that respect, during the writer's recollection; they may have had equals. The dogs of pre-trial days were for the most part unbroken, the dogs we shoot over today are mostly broken. Herein lies the difficulty of comparing them. The average Retriever or Spaniel to be seen in the shooting field now is quite unlike the dog usually seen forty years ago. He has been evolved to suit the average shooting man, who is not a dog breaker and must have a steady dog which requires no looking after. A dog of this kind must of necessity be lacking in enterprise and drive to some extent, and cannot be compared with the best of our Field Trial performers. A dog which never gets out of hand, whatever liberties are taken with him, is, it must be admitted, unlikely to be a very high class worker. Dogs of this class are, however, in the majority at the present time, and are moreover most sought after. How can one compare these quiet, well behaved, fairly efficient Retrievers and Spaniels with the dogs the writer first remembers? They had never proved their ability to be broken. What would they have been like had they been broken? Would they have retained all the drive and game finding ability which many of them undoubtedly possessed? Would they have given as much satisfaction to the average shooting man as the dogs he is now provided with? These questions can never be answered and opinions will no doubt differ. It is unlikely, however, that there are many who would be prepared to scrap the dogs of today and return to those of forty years ago.

Even if it cannot be proved that Field Trials have done anything to improve game finding ability, it is certainly true that they have set up a standard of education unthought of before they were instituted. More important still, they have very greatly increased the number of competent teachers. The writer is convinced that upbringing and education come first in importance where gundogs are concerned. There are very few bad dogs born, but want of sympathetic upbringing and mistakes in training are responsible for most of the failures we see about. The importance of breeding must not be overlooked but Field Trials have greatly simplified this question. Most of the best dogs in the country appear at some time in these competitions, and can be seen by anyone desirous of breeding, or selected from the published reports of Trials.

It may fairly be claimed that Field Trials have been instrumental in saving much of the pain which is inevitably caused during a day's shooting. Though it may be that

before the days of Trials there were dogs as capable of finding game as any to be seen today, it is quite certain that
few, if any, of them could be taken out shooting unless
attached by some contrivance to their masters. The consequence was that the keeper's dog was often the only one
out. At the present time it is not uncommon to find eight or
ten dogs hunting for dead and wounded game after each
drive. Furthermore, the keenness of Field Trial competition
is having a marked effect on the average standard of ability
to be found throughout the country. At one time a dog
might fail several times and still be placed first, but at the
present time it is seldom that a dog against which a failure
has been registered can win an Open Stake.

As the number of breakers and owners of shooting dogs
has increased so has the small rough shoot gained in popularity. Few of us, without a dog, would work cheerfully all
day for perhaps a couple of rabbits. Yet accompanied by a
Spaniel or Retriever or two much pleasure is got out of the
smallest of bags. The owner of a Field Trial competitor
would seem to be in a much better position than the owner
of a racehorse. The owner of the former, even if not also the
breaker, can watch and take an intelligent interest in its
training; the Stake in which it is entered often lasts a whole
day or more, and when its Field Trial career is ended a
valuable, well broken, shooting dog is left. The racehorse
owner on the other hand sees little of its training. Any race
in which it may run must be over in very few minutes, and
when its racing career is ended it is of little use except
for breeding purposes. When the cost of the two sports
is compared the dog owner seems to get the most for his
money.

There is little doubt that competitions for gundogs will
increase in popularity and spread to other parts of the
world. The extent of the good they will continue to do
depends largely on the judges. There is only one danger,
though a remote one, ahead. If Field Trials ever become
solely a medium for making money, it will be a bad day for
them. If the men and women who now run dogs chiefly for

102

the sport of it, for the pleasure of breaking, or for the excitement of watching their dogs in competition with others, were to give up competing, Trials would be doomed. As a class, there are no better sportsmen than professional handlers and dog breakers, and many of them show a good example to amateurs in the cheerful way in which they take their defeats, and in their modesty when successful. Every day the number who get their living directly or indirectly through Field Trials increases. So long as the newcomers uphold the traditions of the professionals of the present day all will be well. It must be remembered, however, that it is far harder for a man whose livelihood may depend on it to take an adverse decision, or run of bad luck, in a sportsmanlike spirit, than it is for the average amateur.

In conclusion it may be well to point out that Field Trials are not conducted exactly in the same way as is an ordinary day's shooting, any more than the Grand National resembles a day's hunting.

Field Trials are not intended to be easy, but take place in order to provide tests on which judges have to decide the merits of competitors. The higher the standard which can be arrived at the less will be the suffering inflicted in the shooting field.

A few comments from *Retriever Training* on the subject of the influence of Field Trials might be appropriate here.

Mrs June Atkinson and the late Mrs Audrey Radclyffe both considered that judges often pay too much attention to fault finding rather than judging in a more sympathetic manner by looking for virtues. They would not eliminate a dog for one small squeak or for hard mouth unless the evidence was overwhelming. The latter view was shared by the late Eric Baldwin, who stated that a dog should never be put out of a Trial for hard mouth unless the judges have seen where the bird fell.

When asked how he thought Field Trials had changed over the years, Alan Thornton replied that the top handlers do a lot of work on game, but some of the others do not, and it shows. The top dogs are very good indeed, but those at the bottom end of the scale can be pretty rough.

The Halsteads expressed rather similar views. They think there is better handling but poorer game finding in the majority of dogs. The top ones are very good indeed, probably better than they have ever been, but there are more sub-standard ones about now. They also think that there is less sportsmanship than there used to be and fewer good manners.

Since these conversations took place, the situation has continued to deteriorate. Let us all try to swing the pendulum back before it is too late.

Index

judges failure to see 96–7
judges walking up 6
judging, equity in 11–20
judgment, errors of 34, 84

*Kennel Club Guide to the
    Conduct of Field Trials* 6
Kennel Club Guide to Judges 60
Kennel Club help re dates of
    trials 3–4
Kennel Club rules 7
knowledge gained on previous
    occasions 12–13

Labradors 62, 67
lacerations on game 23
Layerbrook Guinea 32–3, 54,
    93
line,
    dogs not in the 49–50
    positions in the 5, 13
    standing clear of the 74
    taking the 90–92
    walking in 34
luck 11–12, 83

Male, Dick 34, 80
Manymills Drake 57
Manymills Encore 33
Manymills Heron 71
Manymills Lucky Charm
    70–71
Manymills Milady (Millie) 60,
    61, 71, 72
Manymills Tanne (Quinta) 33,
    62–3, 71
marking, bad 78–9
marking the fall 69, 79–80, 81
marks, remembering 19–20
Millie (Manymills Milady) 60,
    61, 71, 72
mistakes by judges 34, 84
mouths, hard 21–6, 41, 70, 103

mustard, recovery of runners
    in 65

natural ability 40–44, 47, 71
noise from dogs 80, 93–4, 96
nose 41, 46, 52–8, 62, 100 *see
    also* scent
notes taken 15
novice judges 79, 81
numbers shown 8

organisation and running of
    Field Trials 3
Ormewood Penny 32

pace 41, 66, 67–8 *see also* drive
pace of the return 28–9, 33
partridges 56–7, 65, 98–9
performance of dogs 15, 97
Peter of Faskally 99
pick up, the 27–8
positions in the line 5, 13
Purbrick, Daphne 31, 47

Quail of Gunstock 83
quartering 69, 95
Quinta (Manymills Tanne) 33,
    62–3, 71

rabbits 84
rabbits, scent of 64
rabbits caught by Spaniels
    94–5
racehorse owners 102
Radclyffe, Mrs Audrey 34, 103
Rawlings, Paul 32
retrieve, crossed 37
Retriever Training 61, 103
Retrievers, Golden 29, 67
Retrievers, water tests for
    75–6
retrieving 27–31
return, pace of the 28–9, 33